Facing Our
Differences

Alan A. Brash

Facing Our Differences

The Churches and Their Gay and Lesbian Members

Risk
BOOK SERIES

WCC Publications, Geneva

Cover design: Edwin Hassink

ISBN 2-8254-1165-5

© 1995 WCC Publications, World Council of Churches,
150 route de Ferney, 1211 Geneva 2, Switzerland

No. 68 in the Risk Book Series

Printed in Switzerland

Table of Contents

Foreword

Of the nearly seventy books which have appeared in WCC Publications' Risk Book Series since 1978, perhaps none has corresponded as well to the title of the series as this one. Several churches are caught in painful and divisive debates on homosexuality. In many cultures, and in the mainstream of Christian tradition, homosexuality has been and still is considered a very serious moral aberration. Until recently, it was even regarded widely as a criminal offence. The moral foundations of social life had to be protected against such destructive influences. Even though many states have in recent decades changed their legislation and decriminalized homosexuality, it remains a very sensitive issue in the public moral consciousness.

Given this situation, why run the risk of entering this very controversial debate? Would it not be advisable to stay out of a discussion which, because of the strong convictions opposing each other, is not likely to lead to any agreement in the foreseeable future and could in fact become a major burden for the ecumenical fellowship? What could be the special contribution of a publication in this series compared with other literature on the subject? Should visibility be given to an issue which is considered by a large number of member churches as totally unacceptable and even a threat to ecumenical fellowship?

These questions have been considered carefully. The decision to commission and finally to publish this manuscript should not be taken as a definitive and programmatic response to such questions. In fact, the questions have to be kept open if an honest debate is to take place.

The present book, as the first chapter makes clear, grows out of an effort among the staff of the World Council of Churches to come to a better understanding of the issues at stake in the debate about homosexuality. After an unexpected and highly controversial discussion at the meeting of the WCC central committee in Johannesburg in January 1994, general secretary Konrad Raiser spoke to the committee of his own responsibility "to make every effort to maintain our fellowship in the face of sharp differences of conviction" and "to manifest pastoral sensitivity" regarding divisions among the churches about "theological and ethical issues of human sexuality and sexual orientation". He was convinced that it would be helpful in this connection for the WCC staff to consider together how they might fulfil their role as facilitators of ecumenical dialogue on this issue. This led to the invitation to Dr Alan Brash, a former deputy general secretary of the WCC, to conduct three staff workshops. At the end of these workshops he presented a paper with his personal assessment, which many of those present found very helpful. The paper was shared with a wider group of persons, especially members of the WCC central committee, to obtain their reactions and their advice whether a book in the Risk series along these lines could be envisaged. The response was encouraging enough to go ahead with the plan. What follows is thus a further development of the presentation made by Alan Brash at the conclusion of the workshops. It is important also to emphasize here the nature and purpose of books appearing in the WCC Publications Risk Book Series. Each of these books addresses an ecumenically important theme or subject through the personal thinking of a single author. To be sure, while writing as individuals, the authors chosen are persons who have demonstrated a broad familiarity with the life of the churches and a commitment to the goals of the ecumenical movement. But in writing a Risk book they are not expected either to survey the full range of discussion on the issue being treated or to propose an ecumenical consensus more or less along the lines of their own convictions about the subject. Rather, the object is to facilitate or advance a discussion within the constituency of the WCC. In fact, enabling the churches to encounter one another in dialogue at those points where sharply contradictory convictions divide them is one of the primary purposes for the existence of the WCC itself.

Alan Brash's international ecumenical career and, as is evident in Chapter 1, his own pastoral experiences have especially qualified him to contribute a Risk book on this subject; and we owe him a debt of gratitude for his willingness to undertake it. At the same time, it is inevitable, given the controversies in the churches surrounding the subject of homosexuality, that what follows is likely to meet with varied responses within the ecumenical fellowship. It is to be expected that readers whose cultural and theological context, life experiences and personal convictions differ from those which shape what Alan Brash has written will diverge from his conclusions, no matter how tentatively they are put forward. Some readers may have wished for a book which treated in a different way or at greater length certain facets of the issue or certain convictions which have been deeply held within the Christian community over the years and around the world. The book will not meet the expectations of some who as Christian gay men or lesbian women are personally concerned, and it will go too far for others who still find it difficult to acknowledge the challenge of homosexuality for the life of the churches and their ecumenical fellowship.

Yet this book is published in the belief that it makes a thoughtful ecumenical contribution to a discussion which is already going on. The divergent reactions to it will underscore the fact that the ecumenical fellowship is far from the point of being able to identify convergences on the issue of homosexuality, much less to make declarations for policy guidance. It is clear that other voices must be heard; and further WCC publications, within or outside of the Risk series, may prove to be an appropriate vehicle for that.

Besides reflecting the nature of the unity being sought by the ecumenical movement, the WCC's vocation to maintain ecumenical fellowship in the face of divisive issues grows out of the recognition of an ongoing pastoral responsibility. That pastoral responsibility in this case includes a readiness to share the burdens of those members of the ecumenical community who are confronted with the issue of homosexuality in their own lives and struggle to find a responsible answer. Any such answer obviously has wider ecumenical implications. The pastoral task implies finally a willingness to acknowledge the experience of those members of the body of Christ who as gay men and lesbian women suffer discrimination and exclusion in church and society and who long for mutual acceptance in the Spirit of Christ instead of condemnation.

As the search goes on for ways to bring all the divergent voices responsibly into this conversation, it will be helpful to take into account reactions from the readers of this book. Such responses, addressed to WCC Publications, P.O. Box 2100, 1211 Geneva 2, Switzerland, will thus be welcome and are, indeed, encouraged.

JAN H. KOK
Publications Manager
Geneva, September 1995   World Council of Churches

Preface

Every Christian church in every land acknowledges that it is called by Jesus Christ to be at one with all other Christians "that the world may believe". The ecumenical movement today is a sign that many churches are struggling to be obedient to that call.

One of the areas on which the churches are not at one, and over which there is either an austere silence or a heated debate, is the understanding of human sexuality, and particularly the aspect of it indicated by the word "homosexuality". The radically different views of this within the churches are not only based on diverse biblical interpretations and theological principles, but are infused with emotion, cultural traditions and prejudice. In combination, these factors are so powerful that they can and do threaten such unity of the ecumenical fellowship as has been achieved.

This modest book is written out of the experience of the World Council of Churches, but it is in no sense an attempt to move that ecumenical body to take any official position on this subject. That is currently impossible. Rather, I have tried here to look at some of the issues involved in such a way that, while my views on many matters are certainly not "neutral", the book will raise some central questions that urgently need to be discussed within and between the churches. My purpose will have been achieved if such open discussion is increased, if some of the emotional inhibitions can be overcome, and if the theological, ethical and biblical principles can in some degree be clarified. The book makes no pretence of being an academic treatise, but rather intends to be a contribution to a highly sensitive but necessary conversation. My reflections are offered not in the spirit of a theological debate, but in a context of prayerful worship.

In the process that has led up to the production of this book I have become indebted to more people than can be mentioned by name. Priority among my expressions of thanks must go to the considerable number of people who have shared with me something of their inner experience in discovering their own sexual orientation. Second, I want to pay tribute to St Ninian's congregation, in Christchurch, Aotearoa New Zealand, for challenging me to take an active part in the struggle for justice in both the country and the Presbyterian Church. They made me study, think and pray very hard indeed. Then I want to acknowledge a great debt to the World Council of Churches, which over the years has enabled me to learn something of the life of Christians in different cultures and with different theologies, and especially to the Rev. Dr Konrad Raiser and his staff for challenging me and assisting me in so many ways to enter this particular study and conversation in the ecumenical field. Obviously I — and all who read this book — are indebted to Aruna Gnanadason, Cristina Boesenberg, Gae and Joleen Cherry, Clive Pearson and Ralph Knowles for their contributions to this book. I have benefited greatly from the editorial skills of John Bluck, Dean of Christchurch Cathedral, and of my daughter Lyn, who helped me to tap the mysterious powers of the word-processor. Finally, I want to acknowledge my great debt to Bob Scott, without whose irritating persistence and personal loving support this book would never have appeared. Further indications of my indebtedness will become clear in later chapters.

If I can also dare to do so, I would like to thank in advance anyone who will respond to this presentation, not in vague praise or in overall condemnation, but in a positive and openly sharing way which will increase our ecumenical understanding of one another both as churches and as individuals. We must find Christian ways to deal with a situation in which a multitude of people in every land are suffering an inner misery and a social rejection which in no way reflects the spirit of our Lord Jesus Christ.

ALAN A. BRASH

1. A Personal Journey

When one dares to write on the subject of sexuality — and homosexuality in particular — it is appropriate to begin by letting readers know something of one's own background, for it is clear that one's views (and prejudices) have been created or substantially qualified by a particular religious and cultural context and the ways in which the elements of that context were interpreted in one's own family.

I am a Presbyterian minister from Aotearoa New Zealand, and was brought up in that country. The family and the congregation in which I grew up moulded all the best things in my life, for which I am profoundly grateful. But despite much that was enriching about that environment, it was such that on the rare occasions when sex was mentioned, it was always in the context of its being evil. The only instruction I actually remember getting regarding my sexual organs was "as far as possible, don't touch". Homosexuality was certainly never mentioned at all, and I grew up in virtually total ignorance of its existence.

I spent some years attending a church school and then a reputable state secondary school, but I do not have the slightest recollection of sexual matters ever being mentioned by my teachers. Of course, sex was a frequent topic of amusement on the school grounds, but while I found these conversations somewhat informative, the way the topic was treated reinforced the guilt implied at home: "sex is dirty; decent people don't talk about it and are never seen to express it."

Much the same can be said of my four years at Otago University in Dunedin, where I took a master's degree in philosophy, and the three years I spent in Scotland studying theology in New College, Edinburgh. As far as I can recall, I received no guidance at all regarding human sexuality — if I had, I am certain that I would remember it, in view of the deep embarrassment it would have caused me at the time.

In the service of the ecumenical movement in later years, I visited churches in some seventy countries, living for some years in Singapore, London and Geneva. Yet although being strongly influenced by a generally Western European cultural tradition, in which many churches have had profound and open debates on the issues of homosexuality, my own background gives me a degree of empathy with Christians in churches where such matters are not mentionable.

When I entered the parish ministry in my native country, I had no experience or qualifications for responding to the many personal problems I was about to meet — including a serious case of incest, family child abuse and marriage problems in general. Though I had come through what was reputed to be a first-rate educational system and held a degree from one of the world's most admired Protestant theological colleges, my education had been one in which sexuality was totally ignored. To remedy this situation, my wife and I read all the books that were available to us; and we trained with the newly formed Marriage Guidance Council of New Zealand — a body considered very suspect by many people at the time. Much later, our grandchildren helped to lead us into a radically more open attitude to sexual matters in general. I remember well the salutary — if somewhat startling — experience it was when our teenage grandson sat down to dinner in our retirement home one day and cheerfully opened the conversation with the expectant question, "Grandma, what do you think about rape in marriage?"

Looking back, I acknowledge with considerable shame that it has only been in the years of my retirement that I have been individually and specifically confronted by the issues of homosexuality in very personal terms. Some of the people whom I most respect and love have shared with me that they are of homosexual orientation and have spoken of the agonizing problems that this creates for them in their personal relationships and social life and in the congregations of many churches. For me, these experiences have been more mind-shattering than any theoretical discussion of the issues could ever be. It has been confirmed to me again and again that discussions on the topic of homosexuality have little value unless the participants are personally aware that they are not talking of abstract ideas but of actual people, many of whom they know and admire. For whether we recognize it or not, discussions about homosexuality are about people — some of whom we see as evil, some as good and, as in other groups, some as both good and evil.

Four years ago I became a member of St Ninian's congregation in Riccarton, Christchurch. I soon discovered that it is a congregation deeply involved in the debate about people of homosexual orientation.

One facet of this involvement has been participating in the political discussion of the laws of the country regarding discrimination. For more than a hundred years, New Zealand had simply followed the long-standing British pattern in which male homosexual relations were illegal and people of that orientation had no protection against discrimination. The matter had been raised in the early 1960s but no change was made at that time. In 1985 amendments were proposed to both the Crimes Act (to decriminalize homosexual relationships under agreed conditions) and the Human Rights Act (to outlaw discrimination against homosexuals). After a heated debate, in which Christian voices, like others, were sharply divided, the former was passed, but the latter was rejected. Then in 1993, a law was passed protecting both people of homosexual orientation and people carrying HIV infection from discrimination in regard to employment and accommodation with minor exceptions.

The substantial majority by which the 1993 law was passed gave evidence of the considerable change in public opinion, as well as among members of Parliament, which had taken place during those seven years. In the whole period of intense debate, St Ninian's congregation was vocal in support of the proposed law changes. It presented its views to the special committee set up by the government to hear submissions from the public.

At the same time, the congregation was becoming increasingly involved in the debate within the Presbyterian Church of Aotearoa New Zealand. In 1985, when the general assembly of that church declared that "homosexuality is sin", St Ninian's was one of a small number of congregations publicly to dissociate itself from that decision (reference to later actions by the general assembly will be made in another chapter). Furthermore, St Ninian's believed that while the discussion was going on at the national level, the congregation should take its own initiative locally as well.

Recognizing that many people, particularly those of my age group, had never really thought through these issues in terms of their faith, the congregation set up a group to produce study resources, not so much to promote a particular view as to lead people through the biblical and other material necessary for making a Christian response. If, as was hoped, the material produced was helpful for the people of St Ninian's, it could also be shared with other congregations.

The group included a gay man, the mother of a lesbian woman, several people of various ages whose background was similar to my own, the local minister — and I found myself named as convenor. Nothing makes me work harder on any issue than being given responsibility for a group that is expected to produce material for the guidance of others; moreover, I am indebted to Clive Pearson, then minister of St Ninian's and now professor of systematic theology in the Theological Hall of our church and senior lecturer at Otago University, who took over the convenorship of the group while I was on an extended trip overseas. Eventually we published a study book entitled *The Call of Christ — Good God, They're Gay!*, which has been widely used within Aotearoa New Zealand and elsewhere. Much of this book is based on that material.

Among other places, the St Ninian's booklet found its way into the hands of some staff members of the World Council of Churches in its headquarters in Geneva, Switzerland. Some of the WCC's member churches have been struggling desperately with theological and policy issues related to homosexually oriented people; other churches, for theological or cultural reasons, have a strong reluctance to discuss the matter at all. While it is impossible for the WCC itself to take an official position on this subject, it is the conviction of Konrad Raiser, the general secretary, that the churches need to be able to talk openly together on these topics, even though they do not agree upon them. Disagreement without dialogue will erode the fellowship for which the WCC was created. Moreover, he recognized that the senior WCC staff, who deal with all those churches in which such a diversity of views prevails, must be fully aware of the theological, biblical and ethical questions involved and able to separate those questions from the emotions and prejudices which affect us all without exception in this area.

On the basis of the St Ninian's booklet and my own familiarity with the WCC, which I once served as a deputy general secretary, I was invited to serve as a facilitator for three three-hour workshops in July 1994 which were designed to equip staff members to discuss the issue of homosexuality openly among themselves and to talk responsibly about it and the churches' reaction to it in their dealings with member churches. Following the workshop sessions, I was invited to present a purely personal paper on the subject for the staff of all the organizations in the Ecumenical Centre in Geneva. This book draws on all that work.

Some people have argued that this issue is so divisive, both between and within the churches, that it should be ignored in the life of the WCC. Many of them would add, with considerable emphasis, that there are far more important issues on which conversation is more urgently needed.

While it must be acknowledged that the WCC is not likely to reach a consensus on the topic of homosexuality in the foreseeable future, there are nevertheless very important reasons why this issue should not be ignored. Moreover, much can be achieved by such a discussion even assuming a continued state of disagreement. Since long before the founding assembly of the WCC in Amsterdam in 1948, the churches have been debating the legitimacy of Christians' engaging in warfare. Certainly no agreement has been reached out of these ecumenical discussions, but there has been a considerable gain in mutual understanding and respect as a result of the truly open exchange of ideas and insights. A similar thing can be said of the ongoing ecumenical debate on the ordination of women to the ministry. There is no unanimity, but there is far more understanding than if the issue had been ignored.

Regarding all matters discussed ecumenically it is always understood in the WCC that when there is a lack of agreement there is no suggestion of imposing a majority view on a dissenting minority. But it is also assumed that continuing the debate in the fellowship of the Holy Spirit will be mutually constructive. Behind the writing and publication of this book lies the clear conviction that the deep and enduring differences of opinion in the churches on the subject of homosexuality will do far less harm if we can share our views responsibly and listen to one another rather than allowing the issues to fester in silence.

If such conversation is to be constructive, it must be remembered that it is not about different attitudes towards gay and lesbian people as if they were a group only outside the churches. There is a very significant number of such people within all the churches, and they often have important insights to share coming from their own experiences and approach to Scripture. If our conversation is to serve justice as well as demonstrate openness, those insights must be listened to with a respectful acknowledgment so that they may add further light to our understanding of the nature of the gospel and of the church.

Nearly all the churches involved in the current discussion of homosexuality are in the generally Western tradition; and, as we have said, a great many other churches have considerable resistance to discussing it at all. One purpose of this book is to make an urgent appeal to the latter to face openly the presence in their churches and societies of a substantial number of people who, because of a sexual orientation which they did not choose, are living lives of great anguish with little if any support from their churches. At the same time, this is a painful discussion for all churches without exception, precisely because it is not primarily a theological debate about certain ideas but a pastoral debate about people who are personally suffering and who are often victims of social injustice. These people are paying the price for our ecumenical silence and the indecision of individual churches, and they are being denied the full ministry of our Lord Jesus Christ. Although many of them with amazing faithfulness perform great service at all levels in all the churches, multitudes of others have felt so rejected that they have left the churches entirely.

While not always constructive and seldom sustained, an ecumenical conversation about sexuality has surfaced from time to time in WCC publications and documents. As far back as 1958, at the central committee meeting in Ibadan, Nigeria, one of the group reports drew attention to the relation of the Christian concept of marriage to certain African cultural customs, such as female circumcision, bride price and the treatment of widows. In 1966 the WCC's world conference on Church and Society discussed in considerable depth the relationships of women and men in changing societies, including issues of divorce and sterilization. At the Uppsala assembly (1968), a report entitled "Towards New Styles of Living" was commended to the churches for study and action. It covered a variety of "life-style" issues; and the section on "Creative Partnership" included the following recommendation:

> Family patterns change in different social settings, and Christian marriage can find its expression in a variety of ways. We would like materials elaborating the problems of polygamy, marriage and celibacy, birth control, divorce, abortion, and also of homosexuality, to be made available for responsible study and action.

While this statement marked an exception to the consistent avoidance of any reference to homosexuality in international ecumenical circles, and although in the years that followed homosexuality and the other issues mentioned here were indeed on the agenda of many individual churches, no substantial ecumenical discussion of such questions resulted.

In May 1978 *One World*, the monthly magazine of the WCC, published a significant article entitled "Red Hot and Rock Cold", which illustrated clearly what was said earlier: that the debate on the church and homosexually oriented people is intense in some parts of the world and persistently ignored in others. However, the article disputed the idea that this debate was taking place only in liberal, "mainstream" Western churches, noting that strong caucuses existed within Seventh-day Adventist, Mormon and Jewish communities. In Latin America churches were reported to deal with the matter privately, while considering homosexual activity a heinous sin. The reporter from Latin America quoted a press interview with a Brazilian writer who put the number of homosexuals in Brazil alone at eleven million. In Africa, the article observed, homosexuality remained a taboo subject in both church and secular society.

One of the eight "issue groups" at the WCC's Vancouver assembly in 1983 included the following among its recommendations: "That the churches be encouraged to examine and study for themselves and with one another the question of homosexuality, with special stress on the pastoral responsibility of the churches everywhere for those who are homosexual." Although this recommendation did not mandate any specific action by the WCC (which is the responsibility of the central committee), it clearly went further than the Uppsala report, reflecting a somewhat increased openness to facing issues of sexuality in the context of the ecumenical movement. In large measure this

8

grew out of the sustained attention within the WCC to the relationship between women and men in church and society. During the years preceding Vancouver this had been focussed in the study on the Community of Women and Men in the Church, culminating in the Sheffield conference of 1981. Issues of prostitution and rape were freely discussed, along with sex tourism, which was described as "a sign of degrading human exploitation, linking sex, class and race in one web of oppression". Careful attention was given to understanding the place of women in the cultures reflected in the Bible.

In 1983, Marie Assaad, staff moderator of the WCC unit on education and renewal, initiated a two-year interfaith study to examine the extent to which religious teachings relating to female sexuality influence woman's perception of herself and society's perception of her role and status. The study, which was coordinated by the sub-unit on women, grew out of recommendations from the Community of Women and Men in the Church study and from concerns expressed by women at the 1980 UN mid-Decade forum in Copenhagen. The resulting publication *Women, Religion and Sexuality* (J. Becher ed., WCC, 1990) pointed to similarities in the perception of women and female sexuality shared by Buddhists, Hindus, Jews, Muslims and Christians of various confessions. For the WCC this was a pioneer interfaith publication on human sexuality. It has been used by study groups in local situations to raise awareness about religious attitudes towards female sexuality.

The 1984 central committee meeting in Geneva, following the Vancouver assembly, did endorse a recommendation that a study on sexuality and human relations be undertaken, though it again avoided any explicit reference to homosexuality. Responsibility for coordinating the study was assigned to the WCC sub-unit on Education, and it carried out the process over a period of several years in consultation with member churches and related groups. In 1989, when the central committee met in Moscow, it was reported that a draft text had been completed and was being circulated with a questionnaire anticipating revisions. The major concern at that point, however, seems to have been with the economic injustices to which many women are subjected.

The sub-unit on Education eventually did publish a booklet designed to assist churches to do their own studies of sexuality, as recommended at Vancouver. What was produced made no claim to be an authoritative document of the WCC; and the coordinator of the study, Robin Smith, was well aware that it is impossible in such a document to cover all aspects of human sexuality. But the group responsible did at least raise some of the relevant questions for churches in relation to human sexuality, marriage, divorce and remarriage, domestic violence, singleness, homosexuality, abortion and AIDS.

Documents from about forty churches are cited in the study book. In addition, about a dozen responses to the initial draft (mostly from the North, although there were also comments from Brazil, India and Nigeria) were received and taken into account in producing the final version. Yet while this study did indicate a new readiness within some parts of the ecumenical fellowship to take up issues of sexuality together, the strong hesitations also continued. The booklet was not widely advertised or promoted and has remained largely unknown.

Tensions within many churches on the specific issue of homosexuality — which we will survey more extensively in Chapter 3 — have continued to manifest themselves in recent years. They surfaced again in an impassioned debate during the 1994 WCC central committee meeting in Johannesburg over a reference in one of the reports singling out violence against lesbian women as an area of special concern. Against that background, the WCC staff seminars focussing on homosexuality in July 1994 and their follow-up in this book have been designed to carry this whole sensitive conversation one stage further by concentrating on that one area of concern and suffering.

2. The Nature of Sexuality

Every human being has a sexual dimension to his or her nature. That dimension may vary in strength between one person and another, and at different times in the life of an individual, but it is always present from birth to death; and we can surely say that it is a feature of how we are made. This sexual dimension is the physiological and psychological reality which draws us into close relationships with other human beings, whether those relationships are expressed in a very temporary way, in a purely physical way or in a comprehensive relationship of enduring love. The church, following conventional wisdom, has traditionally seen the beginning of sexuality at puberty, but it is increasingly accepted that sexuality is a part of every human being from birth. Research at Johns Hopkins University in the US has suggested that the particular orientation of a person is fixed by the age of two years.

Sexuality is the way of reacting to the world as a male or a female. It is what calls people out of themselves into associations with other people. As such it is a factor influencing every aspect of a person's life. While it is clear that the sexual dimension of life includes the procreation of children, few people today would claim that this is its only function.

Any discussion of sexuality inevitably raises questions about the nature of "the body", with its impulses, needs and functions, and of what is often referred to as "the spirit", seen as a separate and distinguishable reality. The issue of "body" and "spirit" — the definition of and distinctions and relations between the two — is the subject of an old and complex philosophical discussion. For our purposes here it is enough to observe that popular thinking on this matter is often oversimplified and superficial and that our assumption in this book is that a human being is a body-spirit unity. Our sexuality is part of that total unity.

Although sexuality is a universal characteristic of all human beings, it is a very difficult subject for many people to discuss, for at least two reasons. First, everyone grows up in a particular cultural background. Even if there is perhaps nobody who identifies completely with his or her cultural background — for every person is an individual — no one entirely escapes it either. From the moment of birth one imbibes the attitudes of that culture, including its attitudes and inhibitions with respect to sexuality in all its aspects. In many cultures, in fact, there is a conspiracy of silence on the whole topic. A whole system of rules emerges to cover the expression of sexual interest.

Second, as persons develop they gather into their emotional nature certain strong desires and inhibitions regarding particular types of sexual expression. Many adults are totally repelled by the thought of oral intercourse, for example, but for other people it is a joyous expression of intimacy. Such emotional feelings — and they are many — influence each person's life and the kind of intimate relations he or she can or cannot develop.

For these reasons, in discussing the whole topic of sexuality ecumenically, we must advance slowly and considerately if we are to learn from one another individually and as churches.

The sexual reality for the majority of people is an attraction they feel for persons of the opposite sex. For a considerable number it can also be felt, for a shorter or longer period in their lives, as an attraction towards and a desire for intimate contact with either people of the opposite sex or people of the same sex. For a minority of people, both men and women, the sexual reality is expressed lifelong only as an attraction to people of the same sex as themselves.

It is not necessary here to discuss in detail sexual attraction in the majority heterosexually oriented group. The second group is exemplified by the number of people whose marriages break down, and then one or the other partner turns not to another person of the opposite sex but to someone of the same gender. Such people appear to have some degree of choice in the matter of sexuality. In the case of the third group, who feel an attraction only towards people of the same sex, this is not a matter of choice. It is the way they are made. It is with this third group that we are concerned in this book, although it is clear that many urgent concerns arise from other aspects of the expression of human sexuality. Nor should the discussion of homosexually oriented people take place without the involvement of people who are bisexually and heterosexually oriented.

In every human society known to history there have been people drawn to intimate sexual relations with others of the same sex. As we look at societies and cultures of the past, it is almost impossible to assess the proportion of same-gender sexual relations that existed among the vast majority of unnamed people in those societies, and it is unwise to speculate.

What is not speculative, however, is the extent to which intimate same-gender relations were engaged in by certain figures of whom history has recorded a great deal.

Same-gender intimacies were widely accepted in Greek and early Roman centuries. Plato, for example, especially in his earlier years, clearly preferred love-making with another man to that with a woman. Historian Edward Gibbon wrote that only Claudius among the first fifteen Roman emperors had "a normal taste in lovemaking". Down through history, whatever the status of same-gender relations has been in the eyes of the law, a succession of great artists, writers, soldiers, statesmen, kings and churchmen have left records of having engaged in them. Among famous men and women who are recorded as having engaged in such relationships are Richard the Lion-Heart, Leonardo da Vinci, Michelangelo, Francis Bacon, Christopher Marlowe, Erasmus, Anselm, Dostoevsky, Tchaikovsky, Herman Melville, John Maynard Keynes, Walt Whitman, King James I of England, King Henry III of France, Lawrence of Arabia, Kaiser Wilhelm II, Queen Christina of Sweden, Virginia Woolf, Katherine Mansfield and Greta Garbo.

The US sex researcher Alfred Kinsey claimed, on the basis of a study of fifty thousand people, that 37 percent of men had homosexual contacts at some stage of their lives, 13 percent had more homosexual than heterosexual contacts for at least three years and 4 percent had exclusively homosexual contacts throughout their lives. A recent researcher into Catholic thought estimates that there are ten million irreversibly homosexually oriented men in the USA. Another researcher, Hershfield, in 1913 stated that he believed there were at least 10,000 homosexually oriented people in Germany at that time. But it is virtually impossible to secure reliable figures on which everyone agrees; and those who have engaged in research of one kind or another vary greatly in their estimates of what percentage of humanity is of unchangeably homosexual orientation — from one percent to ten percent. This is illustrated by the fact that the Hong Kong government estimates that from 30,000 to 50,000 of its citizens are of homosexual orientation whereas others claim that the number is as high as 300,000.

Such discrepancies are paralleled elsewhere, obviously because a large number of the people who feel attracted to persons of the same sex keep that fact secret or, to put it colloquially, remain "in the closet".

But no matter which of these estimates is most accurate in fact, there can be no doubt that there are a great many people in every society in the category we are discussing. As C.A. Tripp observes, homosexual people are found in every type of human society: "High, low and intermediate rates of homosexuality are found among people who live in hot or cold climates, who are rich or poor, educated or not, quite irrespective of whether they live in a stone age society or in an advanced civilization."[1] No matter how reliable or unreliable one judges the detailed estimates of numbers to be, it is abundantly clear that there is a serious concern for the churches as to how these people are treated.

It is not our intention here to go into the medical debate about whether the homosexual condition is to be classified as a pathological state. Suffice it to say that medical and psychoanalytical opinion has increasingly departed from that view. Psychological tests do not reveal a higher rate of neurotic conditions among homosexual people than among heterosexual; and the fact that homosexual people have higher rates of suicide and alcoholism is clearly a consequence of the fact that they are often socially rejected and even subject to blackmail.

Only in the nineteenth century were the terms we use today to refer to people drawn to intimacies of a same-gender variety clarified. For example, the basic concept of "sexual orientation", first proposed by a Swiss doctor in 1869, has been commonly used in Britain only since the Wolfenden Report in 1957. It is now generally accepted that, whatever the cause, the majority of human beings have an innate "tendency" or "orientation" towards attraction to the opposite sex. Persons in the intermediate group mentioned above can be said to have a "bisexual orientation". And the group we are primarily concerned with in this book can be said to have a "homosexual orientation".[2] Thus it can be said that all human beings have one or other form of orientation. In all cases, that tendency can either be expressed, resisted or, especially in the case of women, repressed by others.

There is no sure way of applying this quite modern terminology — and one can speculate about why it was not discovered earlier — to the famous people listed above to determine whether they were of bisexual orientation or unchangeably homosexual. Of the many of them who were married it is possible to suggest that they were bisexual, but it is equally likely that they were homosexual by orientation but forced into heterosexual marriages by social or other pressures. All we know is that they are reported to have engaged in sexual activities with people of the same gender.

Another important clarification to be made is that our references to homosexual activity in this book are to *adult* relationships. Of course, there are some homosexual men who "interfere sexually" with children, although the majority of those who engage in such activities are in fact heterosexual. Such people are known as paedophiles, and the issues raised by this behaviour are quite different from our focus on the church and persons of completely homosexual orientation.

Inevitably, persons who are heterosexually oriented pose such questions as: "What is the cause of some people being unalterably homosexual? When did they depart from the majority course?" Many different answers have been attempted to these questions. Some believe that it has something to do with prenatal processes. Others attribute it to some combination of factors in a child's upbringing, including his or her relationship to one or the other parent. The most persuasive explanation — that it is in fact the result of a considerable number of factors — is summarized well by D.J. West: "If any one factor was the cause of homosexuality, it would have been discovered long ago. It is the outcome of a complex interaction between individual needs and dispositions on the one hand, and environmental pressures, constraints and opportunities on the other. And causes vary from person to person."[3] What seems important for the churches to hear is what such persons say of themselves: "We discovered our sexual orientation; we did not choose it; and we cannot change it." If some do change, it is presumably because they are of a basically bisexual orientation.

Let me suggest two important reasons why the questions about original causes, while understandable, are not relevant to the concerns of the churches. First, it is just as appropriate (or inappropriate) to ask, "What is the origin of the heterosexual orientation of the majority of people?" And there is no agreed answer to that question either. From a Christian perspective, it seems fitting to say in response to both questions, "It is the way human beings are made, and they are not all the same." Second, accepting that a considerable minority of human beings are in fact of homosexual orientation, the question of surpassing importance is, "How are we going to show them the love and understanding that every human being needs and longs for?"

Finally, we should acknowledge that there is a powerful and long-standing tradition within Christianity to regard all expression of our sexuality as sinful. The prevalence of this assumption is clearly illustrated by the fact that the phrase "living in sin" is always taken as having a sexual connotation. Often this is supported by reference to biblical texts, some of which we shall look at more closely in a later chapter. Here we need only to note that such texts emerged from a culture in which the naked human body was regarded with abhorrence and from a legal code in which half the sins listed as worthy of death are sexual sins. There is no doubt that our sexual nature — whether heterosexual or homosexual — can be expressed in ways that are evil, unloving and brutal. But it is my assumption and conviction, which is shared by most people of faith, that our sexuality as such is one of the good gifts of God. Obviously it can be debased. It has also sometimes been sacralized, as in the Baal worship against which the Israelites were constantly warned because it involved both disloyalty to Yahweh and male and female prostitution as part of the worship of fertility gods.

Clearly there will always need to be rules which govern when and with whom certain forms of sexual activity are acceptable socially and morally, just as there are similar rules to govern most of the things we do. But the fact remains that the sexual dimension of our personalities is a great, good and enriching gift of God, to be accepted and expressed with love and in no way to be despised.

Any discussion of sexuality among Christians inevitably brings up the issue of the Christian understanding of marriage. While a full discussion of this is beyond the purpose of this book let me state clearly three basic assumptions. First, one of the major purposes of marriage — but not the only one — is the creation of families in which the sexual function of procreation is fulfilled. Second, the procreation of children is not the only purpose of marriage. There is also a lifelong relationship of companionship, mutual support and belonging. A childless marriage is still a marriage, whether it is intentionally or unintentionally childless. A marriage of two people who are beyond child-bearing age is also a true and full marriage, despite the fact that child-bearing is no longer possible within it. Third, sexual intercourse is not confined to the procreation of children, but includes a joyous expression of the total relationship of the marriage. Sexual activity does not of itself create that relationship. The relationship is prior to the sexual expression of it.

Sexuality is an aspect of the whole person, which expresses itself in many ways, of which genital activity is only one. Sexuality is part of our whole personality, and our whole personality is involved in its expression. A useful comparison is verbal communication: when we speak, it is not only our lips and vocal cords that are involved but our whole being; when we write, it is not only the work of our fingers but the communication of our whole person. Sexuality is also the expression of our whole selves, and as such is a great, good and enriching gift of God our creator.

NOTES

[1] C.A. Tripp, *The Homosexual Matrix*, New York, McGraw-Hill, 1975, p.68.
[2] Contrary to a common misconception, the term "homosexual" applies to both men and women. The prefix *homo* is derived from the Greek word for "same", not (as is sometimes believed) from the Latin word *homo*, which means "man" (generally, in fact, in the sense of "human being").
[3] D.J. West, *Homosexuality Revisited*, London, Duckworth, 1977, p.85.

3. The Debate in the Churches

The reason why the topic of homosexuality has become significant for the ecumenical movement and the World Council of Churches is that it is the subject of such heated debate in so many churches. At stake in that debate is the understanding of such central doctrines as the nature of the church, its ministry in the world and the interpretation of the Bible. Lying behind these considerations are even more profound ones concerning the kind of God we believe in and what we believe about Jesus Christ. Such a debate cannot be ignored ecumenically, even though many churches do not at all feel the urgency of it.

In this chapter we shall look more closely at how the issue of homosexuality is being dealt with in a number of church situations around the world. A few qualifications about this material should be mentioned at the outset. In the first place, our purpose here is to indicate by the use of specific examples the shape that the debate is taking, not to offer an exhaustive survey or synthesis of what churches have said or done. Since the debate in many churches has been a long and difficult one, a single action by a church's governing body seldom ends the discussion; and some of the statements quoted or policies described here may have been superseded. Moreover, what is cited or summarized concerning how a particular facet of the issue of homosexuality has been dealt with in a given church may by itself not give a complete or even accurate impression of that church's overall position (if indeed it has taken one).

I shall begin with the events in the church to which I belong, the Presbyterian Church of Aotearoa New Zealand. In 1985 the general assembly adopted a five-part motion whose effect was to:

(a) affirm to homosexuals God's love and acceptance of them as people; and affirm the power of Jesus Christ to forgive, and of the Holy Spirit to transform the lives of all those involved in the homosexual life-style; (b) affirm that homosexual acts are sinful; (c) call the church to initiate compassionate ministry in the power of Jesus to those involved in homosexual life-style; (d) recommend that homosexual acts in private between consenting males over twenty no longer be a criminal offence; (e) call on the government, in the event of legislation to decriminalize homosexual acts, to enact appropriate measures to protect public health and public morality in schools, public places and places of work.

These statements were carried by 135 votes in favour to 114 opposed — of whom 67 felt strongly enough to ask that their personal dissent be recorded. The basic questions at issue in this debate were whether homosexual orientation is always changeable, whether homosexual acts are always sinful, whether private homosexual acts by mutual consent between adult men (no mention was made of acts by lesbians) should be considered a crime and, if not, whether the government should nevertheless place restrictions on homosexually oriented people to protect society and morality.

Over the next six years discussions concerning homosexually oriented people became more intense. On the one hand, there was a public political debate over whether such people should be legally protected from discrimination. On the other hand, controversy within the Presbyterian Church was heightened when David Brommell, a self-acknowledged gay minister, left the Baptist Church and applied for ministerial status in the Methodist Church. While not yet fully accepted as a Methodist minister, he was appointed "supply minister" in a Methodist congregation in Dunedin, where he was warmly appreciated. The reason that this issue in another church worried some Presbyterians was that several years earlier the Presbyterian and Methodist churches had established a mutual recognition of ministers. Thus if the person concerned should be fully accepted as a Methodist minister, he would then be eligible for a call to a Presbyterian congregation.

This stimulation of an already existing debate brought a crisis at the general assembly in 1991. Motions and countermotions, deep divisions and records of dissent abounded. Finally the assembly set up a special committee to consider the issues, consult widely in the church and report back not later than 1995. That decision itself reflected how the pressure of an emotional debate can lead to quite contradictory procedures, for while setting up a special committee to report back in four years it also referred to the presbyteries for a yes-no vote the question of whether self-avowed active homosexual persons should be prohibited ordination. This latter decision meant that a majority opinion could be received and possibly incorporated into the law of the church by 1992, three years prior to the committee's report. The assembly also recorded a detailed statement from those who wanted their reasons for dissent explicitly expressed, as well as a statement from some others in reply to those reasons.

The actions by the church's 25 presbyteries revealed still further the deep divisions of opinion. Thirteen presbyteries supported the prohibition of ordinations or inductions of self-avowed and active homosexual persons, seven were against it, three resolved not to vote on the matter, one had an even division of members and one did not respond. With this majority of one presbytery the assembly was free to support the interim prohibition but was equally free not to do so. It chose the latter course, which meant quite explicitly that the restriction imposed on such appointments in the 1991 assembly had lapsed, pending the decisions which might be taken in 1995.

The special committee appointed to report on issues concerning homosexuality did so just prior to the 1995 assembly. The major recommendations they submitted were that the assembly:

1) ... declare that those of homosexual orientation are to be received as full members of the church on the same basis as anyone else;
2) ... acknowledge the diversity of viewpoint within the church on issues related to homosexuality, and in light of that diversity resolve to take no steps to enact regulations in regard to homosexual people in positions of leadership;
3) ... encourage continuing dialogue and growth within the church on this issue.

Further recommendations suggested procedures for such continuing dialogue.

The recommendations were approved by eight of the eleven committee members; the other three wished to make a distinction between those of homosexual orientation and those in active homosexual relationships, excluding the latter from positions of leadership within the church.

When the assembly met in May 1995, the atmosphere regarding the proposals of the special committee was extremely tense. After long debate, a multitude of notices of motion and a dozen or so conflicting overtures, many concluded that the church was not yet in a position either to make an agreed public statement or to give any instruction to congregations and presbyteries regarding appointments of people to positions of leadership. A proposal that the whole issue, including all related notices of motion and overtures, be referred to the next assembly, and that in the meantime a concerted effort of discussion, listening and prayer be planned in the presbyteries, was carried, though with a substantial minority against it (more than 80 of the 320 commissioners recorded their dissent).

We noted above that developments in the Methodist Church in New Zealand have had implications for the Presbyterian Church because of agreements between the two denominations. Already in 1970 the Methodist conference had adopted a statement on human sexuality which declared that "the key aspect of sex is relationship and therefore the central moral criterion should be one of responsibility. This concern for the effects of our actions on the well-being of others should permeate our lives. It has particular application to sexual expression... An example may be found in stable and affectionate relationships between homosexuals."

While Methodist and Presbyterian committees on public issues jointly approached parliament regarding the homosexual law reform bill which was making the matter of national concern, many Christian groups and individuals were outspoken in the most extreme terms about the government decriminalization of homosexual actions and proposed measures to outlaw discrimination against homosexuals. Gays and lesbians in considerable numbers left the churches.

In May 1990 the issue came to a head in the Methodist Church over the request of David Brommell, referred to earlier, to be received into the ministry. The general purposes committee recommended acceptance of Brommell, but the conference declined. A wide debate took place throughout the church, led on the one side by the conservative Aldersgate Fellowship and on the other by Methodists for Lesbian and Gay Concerns. During this period a number of congregations in Aotearoa New Zealand declared themselves "reconciling congregations". Of the 14 to do so, eight were Methodist.

A firm policy decision on the question of the ordination of homosexuals could not be taken at the 1991 conference because the conference had previously adopted a decision-making process only by consensus and not by majority vote. In the months following, an openly gay minister was inducted into one parish, but Brommell was not received into the Methodist ministry and later went into secular employment. In 1993 the conference agreed to accept what was by that time the law of the country and not to discriminate against a ministerial candidate in either employment or housing on the grounds of sexual orientation.

In turning now to some representative statements of policy and conviction emerging from churches outside of my own country and confessional tradition, I am aware of the risks and difficulties, often evident in ecumenical experience, of giving an account of the theological and ethical beliefs of others, particularly when one must do so on the basis of written (and often only secondary) sources, sometimes in translation. In what follows I have sought to do justice to the information to which I have access and to indicate clearly its sources; and I regret if any inaccuracies or misrepresentations have crept in. Again, it should be remembered that the purpose of citing these examples is to sketch a picture of the debate on homosexuality taking place within and among member churches of the World Council of Churches.

Press stories in November 1994 reported that Patriarch Teoctist, head of the Romanian Orthodox Church, had "sent an urgent message to the members of the Romanian parliament calling on them to resist international pressure to legalize homosexual acts". After the parliament voted down the decriminalization of homosexual acts in October, it came under pressure from the Council of Europe to reverse its decision. In his message the patriarch called for the protection of Romania's "special respect for the family" and described homosexual relationships as "dishonourable love" which the church rejects. [1]

About the same time there were reports that the Evangelical Lutheran Church of Latvia had called homosexual acts "a deadly sin" and instructed its congregations to exclude from the eucharist practising homosexuals who do not repent of their homosexuality. [2] The same resolution also said that "persons deliberately practising homosexuality and having chosen it as their way of life are not allowed to fulfill any duties and positions in the church hierarchy".[3] While the question of the ordination of homosexual persons to the ministry has been a contentious issue in many churches, Lutheran sources reported that the action taken by the Latvian church regarding the eucharist — which is tantamount to excommunication — was without precedent among Lutheran churches worldwide. Some Lutheran observers, in fact, drawing a parallel between the action by the Latvian church and the separation at the communion table according to race of South African Christians during the apartheid era, raised the question of whether this should be seen as a *status confessionis* — a matter on which a difference of opinion warrants breaking fellowship.

An extensive and painful debate has been going on since the 1970s within the Reformed Ecumenical Council (formerly the Reformed Ecumenical Synod) (REC/RES) over the actions and statements on homosexuality by one of its founding members, the Reformed Churches in the Netherlands (GKN) — which, unlike most REC members, is also a member of the WCC. This has been a painful debate because one of the basic tenets of the REC, which brings together conservative churches of Dutch Calvinist and Scottish Presbyterian traditions from around the world, has seemed to be called into question: the authority of Scripture. Yet one of its remarkable features is the seriousness with which most of those on both sides have appeared to be respecting one another as sincere Christians, although in recent years several churches have left the fellowship over the GKN position on this issue.

According to a report in 1980, it was estimated that 4 to 5 percent of the population of the Netherlands is of homosexual orientation, and that many of these persons are members of the GKN. The GKN synod, meeting in Delft in 1979, had called on the churches to "accept the homophile[4] neighbour, to organize dialogue between the homophile and the heterophile members of the congregation and to further the communion of the saints *inter alia* by means of participation in the Lord's Supper and by service in ecclesiastical office". The report went on to say that this decision "evoked serious concern" within the GKN and "shock and distress" among RES member churches. The GKN, added the report, "made no definite pronouncement on the question of whether the homophile orientation is a sin or not and has not distinguished between homophile orientation and homosexual practice. No restraint on homosexual practice is mentioned in the decision." The GKN delegates to the RES clearly considered the Delft statement to be pastoral advice not necessarily involving an ethical judgment, but the majority of the RES feared that it would lead to an increase of homosexual activity, which they regarded as sin. Thus the RES wrote to the GKN to ask for an assurance that no known practising homosexual would be allowed to partake of the Lord's Supper or hold ecclesiastical office.

A report submitted to the GKN synod in 1981 received wide circulation within other Reformed churches. It offered a comprehensive view of the whole subject of homosexual orientation and practice and took a particularly close look at all the relevant biblical passages. In view of the widespread ecumenical discussion, it may be worthwhile to set out the four different perspectives represented among the members of the theological commission which conducted this study.

According to some, the Bible does not allow the experience of homosexual friendship. Therefore, from the pastoral perspective, the living together of homophile persons can be regarded only as a temporary emergency measure.

A second point of view was that because the Bible does not explicitly speak about loving and faithful homophile relations, there can be different opinions among Christians as to whether in such a relationship the actual sexual experience is permissible or not. Opting for the latter is preferable.

The third and fourth positions both begin from the fact that the concept "homophile" as used today does not occur in the Bible. If we take seriously the commandment of love for the neighbour, we must respect the decision made by homophile fellow Christians before the face of God as to whether or not they regard themselves bound by the biblical prohibitions in this area. From this point, some would go on to argue that, although the church on the basis of Scripture may set certain conditions for all relationships among Christians (love, faithfulness, sanctification of life), it should refrain from any kind of ethical pronouncement about whether or not it is permissible for homosexuals to live together.

Others would be less reticent. While agreeing that the biblical prohibition of homosexual relations is clearly shaped by the time and place in which it was written, they would contend that there are situations today so similar to what the Bible rejects that the church may say that in such cases the prohibition remains in force. At the same time, the church is not free to keep silent regarding the permissibility of something about which the Bible does not speak: homophile relationships of love and fidelity, which in fact do justice to the deepest intention of the prohibition passages precisely by safeguarding and fostering the sanctity of life. Of such relationships the church must say that they are permissible even though the Scripture does not speak directly about them.

Among members of the two largest Protestant churches in the Netherlands — the GKN (to which we have been referring) and the Netherlands Reformed Church (NHK) — serious divisions remain on the subject of homosexuality. The GKN, traditionally the more theologically conservative of the two, has officially taken the position that people of homosexual orientation can be fully welcomed into the whole life of the church. In the NHK it has been accepted as a prerequisite for further discussion that, whatever one's sexual orientation and theological conviction, mutual acceptance as fellow members of the church is critical, but no official policy has been adopted. In a number of other Dutch churches the whole issue is receiving close attention although no official action has been taken.

No official statement on homosexuality has been recently issued by the Evangelical Church in Germany. But the matter is heatedly discussed in the churches in relation both to state and church policies. A committee was appointed in September 1993 to work out an official statement for the church, which would include a policy regarding the employment by the churches of people of homosexual orientation. Study papers have been circulated.

The debate on homosexuality has not reached the central committees of the Church of Ireland (Anglican) since the mid-1970s. A statement by the standing committee in 1978 reflects the church opinion as of that date. While supporting the decriminalization of homosexual acts under certain conditions, it does not declare homosexuality acceptable. Certain homosexual acts were decriminalized in Britain by the sexual offences act of 1967, but no such change has been made in either part of Ireland, and the majority of members of the church committee believe that reform in this area should be considered.

The Churches of Christ in Australia report an ongoing low-key effort to involve members in a "study about homosexuality". This originated in a 1972 resolution by the state conference of Victoria and Tasmania which recognized the urgent need for "more widespread information and understanding within the community about homosexuality and the problems homosexuals face". In 1973 plans were made to circulate a pamphlet including papers from a doctor, a minister, a homosexual, a psychologist and a theologian. According to the national secretary, no further conference actions have been taken, but there is growing awareness of the need to recognize the existence of homosexuals within Christian communities, to increase expressions of compassion and understanding for them and to give general support for legislation decriminalizing homosexuality, which has now been done in all states except Tasmania.

In November 1987, the general synod of the Church of England voted to affirm "that the biblical and traditional teaching on chastity and fidelity in personal relationships is a response to, and expression of, God's love for each of us". This was elaborated in four further affirmations:

(1) That sexual intercourse is an act of total commitment which belongs properly within a permanent marriage relationship.

(2) That fornication and adultery are sins against this ideal and are to be met by a call to repentance and the exercise of compassion.

(3) That homosexual genital acts also fall short of this ideal, and are likewise to be met by a call to repentance and the exercise of compassion.

(4) That all Christians are called to be exemplary in all spheres of morality, including sexual morality, and that holiness of life is particularly required of Christian leaders.

In the following years many expressed dissatisfaction and unhappiness with this resolution, and the house of bishops decided to initiate further work which led in 1991 to the publication of a report entitled *Issues of Human Sexuality*. This report contends that while homosexual orientation and its expression do not provide an alternative form of sexuality as complete within the created order as the heterosexual, homosexual people are in every way as valuable to and as valued by God as heterosexual people. Those who sincerely believe from an educated conscience that a homosexual partnership is God's call to them are not condemned. Homosexual orientation is not a bar to ordination or preferment for clergy, but sexually active homosexual relations are. This report is being widely discussed, but it has not yet led to any change in the official position of the church as adopted by the general synod.

Events and developments in several other churches have made the issue more urgent in recent years, and various actions have been taken in response.

The way in which the issue of homosexuality has been dealt with in the United Reformed Church in the United Kingdom is particularly revealing. A feeling of deep pastoral care for people of homosexual orientation and a conviction of the need to understand their situation have been evident; and there has been a clear willingness to facilitate the expression of sincerely held conflicting views. But the experience of this church also reveals that no matter how open the discussion is, it is impossible to avoid questions of practical policy-making. Policy is shaped, whether by open decision or by default, when action must in fact be taken.

In March 1990 a URC working party circulated a document entitled "Homosexuality: A Christian View". While it did not claim to be a unanimous statement of the committee members, much less to represent a consensus of the church as a whole, it did present a very significant viewpoint for discussion. A previous paper on the same subject had elicited widely diverse reactions in the church, and some of this was taken into account in the new document. However, the primary aim was not to achieve an unattainable agreement but to stimulate concern for homosexual people within and beyond the church.

The working party accepted the estimate that about 5 percent of people are inherently homosexual. They agreed that while some people have changed their sexual orientation, others are certainly unable to do so even if they so wished. While rejecting promiscuous homosexual and heterosexual relationships, they were not prepared to say that committed, long-term relationships including sexual love between unchangeably homosexual people are intrinsically sinful. Moreover, they said, the church should openly face the question of blessing such relationships and not simply do so in secret as at present. The working party also confronted the issues of biblical interpretation. In no way, the group insisted, were they questioning the basic authority of the Scriptures; rather, they were discussing how to interpret that authoritative Scripture and apply it to the contemporary situation.

In response to this paper, another (equally unofficial) paper was produced, entitled "Homosexuality and the Gospel: A Contemporary Restatement of Traditional Christian Teaching". While not accepting the conclusions of the first paper, it exhibits a similar pastoral care. This paper seeks to restate what has been "universally held by the church until recent times" in the light of the present state of knowledge regarding homosexuality. Its basic premise is that no one is to blame for his or her sexual orientation, for which many have had no choice. But homosexual acts are in some degree a matter of choice and therefore come under moral judgment. All genital acts outside marriage, including homosexual acts, are sinful, and the Bible is so interpreted. Even if the concept of "sexual orientation" was not understood until relatively recently, the biblical witness against homosexual acts was made in an awareness that this would effectively prohibit any sexual activity for some. Homosexuality is "part of the fallenness of humanity along with our pride, self-sufficiency, lust, selfishness, greed and anything else which falls short of God's glory". The paper is also explicit that "Christians need to abandon their phobias about homosexuality and offer homosexual people the love and support they need to fulfil God's calling for them, whatever it may be" (presumably their only option is total celibacy). "In particular, we need to get rid of the lie that anyone who is homosexually oriented is a pervert and more likely than a heterosexual person to corrupt the young."

Both papers have made important contributions to stimulating discussion and creating understanding within the URC, as they were intended to do. However, the hope of avoiding policy decisions at the highest level has been called into question by the declaration of two candidates for the ordained ministry during the process of assessment that they are gay. Should such students be accepted or rejected solely on merit, or should they be rejected just because they are homosexual, no matter how excellent their general qualifications? Although both candidates have entered ministerial training, the issue has not been resolved and will inevitably come before the general assembly for decision in the future. Meanwhile, a third paper, entitled "Speaking for Ourselves", has been written by a group of gay and lesbian people (who felt compelled to remain anonymous) within the URC. It is a valuable contribution to the discussion, which makes it clear that homosexually oriented people are already present at every level in the church.

The URC established a mission council task group on sexuality "to work out a process whereby the URC can be enabled to hold an informal debate on the matter of human sexuality and come to a decision on the implications for ministry within the church". It recommended that the 1995 assembly not decide on matters of policy but approve a process, including the preparation and discussion of papers on the subject, "by which the church might discuss the ordination of homosexuals in the context of human sexuality as a whole". Assuming that such discussions at all levels in the church will take at least a year, decisions on policy would not be made by the assembly before 1997. In the event, this proposal was endorsed by the URC assembly in July 1995.

The title of a pastoral study document of the house of bishops of the Episcopal Church in the USA is significant: "Continuing the Dialogue". The title reflects an acknowledgment both that several issues are unresolved (as the report correctly notes, "on the subject of human sexuality even the so-called experts do not agree") and that the church's general convention has been unable to deal with the complex issues surrounding sexuality by means of the normal legislative process.

In 1979 the Episcopal house of bishops had accepted a report from its theological commission which stated that "the church is right to confine its nuptial blessing exclusively to heterosexual marriage. Homosexual unions witness to incompleteness." It also recommended that the ordination of "an advocating or practising homosexual is inadmissible". But a minority report was signed by twenty bishops in 1979 and by twenty-nine in 1988. Claiming that Scripture gives no certain basis for a condemnation of homosexual persons or activity, the dissenting bishops indicated their intention not to exclude any person from ordination on the basis of sexual orientation. It is recognized that in reality the church has for centuries ordained gay men and, in more recent years, lesbian women. In 1990, Bishop John S. Spong of Newark, with the consent of the diocesan standing committee, ordained a homosexual person living in a publicly avowed relationship with a person of the same sex. However, the Episcopal Church at present remains unwilling to take legislative action at the highest level.

On the basis of a background paper on "The Church and Homosexuality", the 1978 general assembly of the United Presbyterian Church in the United States of America (which later merged to form the Presbyterian Church, USA) dealt with a variety of issues pertaining to homosexuality, especially the question of the ordination of people of homosexual orientation and practice. The general assembly report stated that "we feel that homosexuality is a contradiction of God's wise and beautiful pattern for human sexual relationships revealed in Scripture". However, it emphasized that "persons who manifest homosexual behaviour must be treated with the profound respect and pastoral tenderness due to all people of God. There can be no place within the Christian faith for the response to homosexual persons of mingled contempt, hatred and fear that is called homophobia." While issuing "definitive guidance" to presbyteries "that unrepentant homosexual practice does not accord with the requirements for ordination", the assembly made it clear that "it would be a hindrance of God's grace to make a specific enquiry into the sexual orientation or practice of candidates for ordained office or ordained officers when the person involved does not take the initiative to declare his or her sexual orientation". Presbyterian seminaries were urged "to apply the same standards to homosexual and heterosexual persons applying for admission". The church committed itself to work for the decriminalization of "private homosexual acts between consenting adults" and called for an end to "the discriminatory enforcement of other criminal laws against homosexual persons". Finally, it declared that these decisions should not be used to "affect negatively the ordination rights" of any deacon, elder or minister who was already ordained.

A 1989 position paper from the doctrinal commission of the Anglican Church of Australia presented its statement on homosexuality in the form of a kind of conversation:

What then can we say to our gay brothers and sisters? Nothing more nor less than we would say to any Christian:

(1) God makes you who you are and who you may become. Your identity rests in your relationship to God, not in your sexuality. Work away at that above all, and let God make you whole.

(2) Learn to accept what you are sexually. Give thanks for your bodies, your physical and emotional make-up.

(3) Let your relationships be governed by the simple precept that you will love your neighbour as yourself.

(4) Consider: Is God calling you to continence or even celibacy as a vocation? In any case, since your bodies are the temple of the Holy Spirit, be careful to express God's love in all that you do, and ask forgiveness when you fail.

(5) Prize faithfulness, openness and permanence in all your friendships.

(6) Seek the support of a Christian community that will accept you and nourish your life in Christ, even if this means walking out of some congregations. However, it might be part of your ministry to persist in the face of rejection.

(7) When life becomes unbearable, for God's sake, talk to someone.

But what are our gay sisters and brothers saying to the rest of us? Four things at least:

(1) Accept us as we are, and listen to what we have to say. Trust that we also seek to follow Christ.

(2) Ask yourself why we homosexuals provoke anger or disgust in you. Is there something you are afraid of?

(3) Don't just debate homosexuality in the abstract. When we meet let us consider the whole question of sexuality and the gospel together.

(4) For Jesus' sake, don't legislate us out of the church. We have a hard enough time as it is. Shouldn't you consider some affirmative and supportive action instead?

While such an attempt to reflect a genuine conversation between those of different sexual orientations is a creative and helpful approach, it is doubtful that this church or any other has yet found the space that would allow a genuine expression of a gay and lesbian theology. Most churches have great difficulty in arranging an open conversation between heterosexual and homosexual people about sensitive areas in the administrative life of the church, far more in hearing the true contribution that those with homosexual orientation might be able to make to Christian theology.

The Uniting Church of Australia expressed its concern about homosexuality by convening a representative group to study the issues. After much research they published "Homosexuality and the Church" in 1985 and invited reactions to it. The response overwhelmed the drafters; and in 1988 they published another pamphlet reviewing the original report and attaching a short summary of the replies and comments to each section. The most common objection revealed by these responses overall was a negative attitude towards what was seen as a somewhat open stance in the original report and towards the way of interpreting Scripture associated with this. The report offered no final verdict on the question of receiving people with homosexual orientation into membership and the ministry. But the committee expressed the opinion that homosexual orientation in itself should not make a person ineligible for membership any more than being heterosexual in itself makes a person eligible. As for ordination to the ministry, the committee's view was that "while a declared homosexual condition should not of itself be a bar to ordination, it is a matter to be taken seriously into consideration, bearing in mind the kind of pressures such a person in ministry would necessarily have to endure". In conclusion, the committee suggested "that it would be inappropriate for any council of the church to try to frame a set of conditions which would spell out precisely which persons should or should not be admitted to membership and ordination. That is for the courts of the church to decide in each case."

In the churches we have looked at so far in this chapter, intensive discussion of matters related to homosexuality has disclosed the presence of diverse opinions deeply and sincerely held. These differences arise not between denominations but within denominations, and the divisions run along generally similar lines in all the churches. To conclude this chapter we shall consider two large North American churches which, while they also contain differences of opinion among their members, have nevertheless made major policy decisions in this area at the highest level.

The situation in the United Church of Christ in the USA is summarized in a document entitled "Social Policy Regarding Lesbian, Gay and Bisexual Concerns", which is a compendium of actions by the denomination's council of social action (1969) and executive council (1973, 1980, 1981), as well as eight general synods between 1975 and 1991. Rather than attempting to offer a detailed summary of this whole series of decisions and actions, we highlight only a few points. On ordination, the 1983 general synod, recognizing that the UCC's polity gives associations the responsibility for ordination and ministerial standing, recommended to associations that "in considering a candidate's qualifications for ministry, the candidate's sexual orientation should not be grounds for denying the request for ordination". As part of a covenant statement, the 1985 general synod declared:

> We know that lesbian, gay and bisexual people are often scorned by the church, and devalued and discriminated against both in the church and in society. We commit ourselves to caring for lesbian, gay and bisexual sisters and brothers by affirming: We welcome lesbian, gay and bisexual people to join our congregations in the same spirit and manner used in the acceptance of any new members.

The United Church of Christ has also witnessed strongly against the "sodomy laws" which make private sexual activity between consenting adults of the same gender a crime in many states of the USA.

The general council of the United Church of Canada approved a major statement on sexuality in 1988 and reaffirmed it in 1992. A central focus was the relationship of homosexuality to the specific matter of church leadership and ordained ministry. Among the elements of this policy are the following:

> (1) All persons regardless of their sexual orientation who profess faith in Jesus Christ and obedience to him are welcome to become full members of the church.
>
> (2) All members of the church are eligible to be considered for ordered ministry. All Christian people are called to a life-style patterned on obedience to Jesus Christ.

(3) It is inappropriate to ask about the sexual orientation of those in the candidacy process or those in the call and settlement process.

The 1992 general council also asked the church's domestic mission division to make available resources for congregations "who wish to proclaim publicly their commitment to being inclusive and welcoming to lesbians and gay men, and to celebrate openly their gifts in the life and ministry of the congregation and community". The general council executive also approved changes in the church's group insurance plan for its employees to allow medical, dental and survivor's benefits to be extended to same-sex partners of church employees, including ministers. Several theological schools related to the denomination have adopted clear anti-discrimination policies in relation to gay and lesbian students.

While a solid majority of general council delegates voted in favour of these policy decisions, it was not unanimous. Following adoption of these policies it appears that about 70 ordained ministers (out of a total of about 4000) have left the denomination. Significant portions of about 60 congregations (out of a total of some 4100 preaching places) have also left. Observers say the departures represent approximately 3.5 percent of the membership of the church. But the policies have not been changed.

All of the churches whose consideration of the issue of homosexuality we have surveyed in this chapter come from the Anglican or Protestant tradition and all are located in Europe, North America, Australia or New Zealand. It is in fact in churches from these confessional and cultural contexts that the overwhelming majority of official ecclesiastical discussions, declarations and decisions about homosexuality have taken place. But it is evident that differences in whether or how the churches in any part of the world are confronting this issue do not mean that the issue itself is less urgent or important.

In concluding this chapter, however, we should underline once more that the brief selection of official actions recorded here is meant to be illustrative. It should not be read as though it were inclusive of all churches which have taken and are taking these issues seriously. More importantly, those churches whose action (or reluctance to act) has been reported in this chapter were not selected because they have emphasized a particular approach to or resolution of this complex and controversial subject. Indeed, the very lack of such unanimity, both within and between churches, serves to accent the importance of seeing homosexuality as an issue on which open ecumenical dialogue may enable the churches to assist each other in their common search to be faithful in our time to the gospel of Jesus Christ.

NOTES

[1] *Ecumenical News International Bulletin*, 94-0115, 21 Nov. 1994, p.12.
[2] *Ibid.*
[3] *Lutheran World Information*, no. 20, 27 Oct. 1994, pp.6f.
[4] Dutch *homofiel*. Although the term "homophile" is not common in English, translations of the GKN statements in RES documents have typically retained it. According to the entry in *Webster's New Collegiate Dictionary* (Springfield, Mass., Merriam-Webster, 1985), which lists the term only as a synonym for "gay", the root "-phile" has the sense of "having a fondness or affinity for [persons of the same sex]".

4. The Sin of Sodom

When Joshua led the Israelites out of their desert life into the promised land, which they slowly conquered, it appears that they found two cities which had been totally destroyed by some cataclysm long before their arrival. Although it is not known today exactly where those two cities were, it is believed that they were in the valley of the Dead Sea, and that their ruins have long since been inundated by its waters. With Israel's intense faith that God controlled the events of history in detail, it became a very important part of its tradition that those two cities had been punished for their great wickedness; otherwise, why were they destroyed?

The tradition about these two cities, Sodom and Gomorrah, was handed down by word of mouth for about a thousand years before it took the written form in which we have it today in Genesis 19. All the major prophets used the example of the two cities to warn their contemporaries of the fate in store for them if they disobeyed the God who had brought them out of Egypt. The New Testament epistles used the same warning, as did Jesus himself. Sodom and Gomorrah became the symbols of the destruction that awaits sin.

The Israelites also wove the city of Sodom into the tradition that revolved around the family of Abraham, who had lived about seven or eight hundred years before his descendants returned under Joshua to claim the land promised to him so long before. They told the story of Lot, Abraham's nephew, who went with his family to live in Sodom, that wicked city. There one day Lot demonstrated the supreme value put on hospitality to strangers. He received two strangers, perhaps angels, into his house for their safety. But the wicked men of Sodom, every single one of them, demanded that the strangers be put outside Lot's house so that they could be abused by a mass rape. In the second century before Christ, long after the time of Joshua and even longer after the days of Abraham and Lot, the idea arose that the sin for which Sodom was destroyed was what we might call same-gender sex. In fact, neither the words of the great prophets, nor of the writers of the epistles, nor of Jesus himself support such an idea. Sodom was the very epitome of the inevitable punishment that comes upon sin — sin which many of the prophets describe in great detail, but never in those terms.

36

The action for which Lot was saved, according to this story from the records of human life long before history was written down, was his obedience to the code of offering hospitality to strangers. When Lot fled Sodom, his sons-in-law stayed with the city and shared its fate. His wife came along, but looked back and was turned into a pillar of salt. From our point of view, living thousands of years later with an entirely different set of values, the real sins in the story are Lot's willingness to offer his two virgin daughters to be mass raped, and the later incestuous relations of those two daughters with him when he was in a drunken stupor after escaping from Sodom. Centuries later, Israel used the account of those incestuous relations to explain the origin of two of its neighbouring nations, the Moabites and the Ammonites, whom they detested.

There are things we can learn from this ancient story, even if it reflects a cultural and religious situation which is very foreign to our contemporary Christian understanding and which we can grasp in only a limited way. But if we want to be true to Scripture, we will look very carefully at the use made of the story by Isaiah, Ezekiel, Amos, Zephaniah, the writer of the Lamentations, the great code of Deuteronomy and by Matthew and Luke in reporting the words of Jesus. Ezekiel, for example, spells out the sins for which Sodom was destroyed: they had wealth and food in plenty, comfort and ease, but never helped the poor and wretched. They violated God's covenant and made light of their solemn oath to God.

Since this ancient story is still used in many churches as proof of divine condemnation of homosexual activity, it is necessary to clarify certain basic points over which confusion has arisen. In the first place, the story is obviously not at all an example of what we now understand as relations between persons of homosexual orientation. What was planned was a mass rape on two men by a mob of men. Since all the men of the city were mentioned, and some emphasis put on that fact, those planning the attack were clearly not only people of homosexual orientation. Still less was it a relationship of mutual consent, but a violation of two people by a mob. Such a mass rape is condemned by every religion and by every known moral code.

But there is an even more subtle confusion which needs to be exposed. It is commonly assumed — understandably, perhaps, though it is not the only possible interpretation — that what was contemplated and what would have happened was a series of attacks by forced anal intercourse. To this day, most heterosexual people assume that anal intercourse is the universal form of lovemaking engaged in by men of homosexual orientation. Throughout human history, many states have not only outlawed anal intercourse but made it punishable by the most cruel forms of death devised by the human mind. Legally, anal intercourse has been called "buggery".

Two facts must be made very clear. First, not all gay men express their sexual relationship in this way, and lesbian women clearly cannot. Second, many heterosexual couples do in fact use this form of intimacy. It is of course true that many heterosexual people have a revulsion to the thought or mention — let alone the practice —of anal intercourse. Many homosexual people share that same revulsion.

What must be remembered is that no form of sexual activity is peculiar to homosexual people. People make intimate sexual love by using one or more of the following techniques — touching, kissing, masturbation, partner manipulation, oral intercourse, anal intercourse and vaginal intercourse. Every person has her or his strong preferences, and that applies to people of all orientations. The laws designed to stamp out "buggery" applied equally whether it took place between people of the same gender or within heterosexual marriage.

If therefore it is granted that rape in the form of anal intercourse was the implication of the Sodom story — and as we have seen this is only one possible assumption — then the word "sodomite" ought properly to be used only of someone who rapes another person by such an action executed without consent and by force. There is no foundation at all for using the condemnation of the proposed action in the account in Genesis 19 as a prohibition of any form of sexual intimacy between consenting adults of the same gender. But many church statements referring to sexual intimacy between two men or two women still turn to this story as a central support for the declaration that all such intimacy is "condemned in the Bible".

Throughout the Bible, Sodom remains a symbol for punishment of sin, though no sexual sin is ever mentioned in this connection. Furthermore, in seeking to understand from a

38

Christian point of view the relevance of this story, we will also have to come to terms with the fact that there is no biblical condemnation of Lot's sin in offering his virgin daughters for mass rape nor of their later incestuous relationships with their drunken father.

To use the word "Sodom" or any of its derivatives to refer to any form of sexual intimacy other than rape by anal intercourse not only misrepresents this ancient story but also ignores the meaning given to this ancient city by Jesus and so many of the great prophets of Israel. All of them refer to Sodom as the symbol for punishment for a great variety of sins, but none of them refers to sexual sins.

5. "It's in the Bible"

Even among people who would admit that their knowledge of the Bible is slight and superficial, there are many who would not hesitate to say that homosexual relations are clearly forbidden in Scripture. On this point many sincere Christian believers who are well acquainted with Scripture would agree with them. In this chapter we shall take a closer look at the biblical texts which are usually referred to in this connection and the different ways in which these passages may be interpreted.

About 15 passages are usually cited in this discussion. Although they are not quoted in full here, it is worthwhile to look them up in the Bible to see exactly what they say and in what context they appear. The texts are:

Genesis 1:27-28 and 2:18-25
Two accounts of the creation of the first man and woman
Genesis 19
The story of Sodom and Gomorrah, which we looked at in the previous chapter; a similar kind of story from the days when Israel had settled in the land of Canaan but did not yet have a king is recorded in **Judges 19**
Leviticus 18:22 and 20:23
Provisions from the so-called Holiness Code regarding sexual morality
Deuteronomy 23:17
A prohibition on the "sons of Israel" becoming temple prostitutes
1 Kings 14:24; 15:12; 22:46; 2 Kings 23:7
Reports of the establishment and abolition of temple prostitution at various times during the period of the monarchy
Romans 1:18-32
A reflection on God's wrath against the "ungodliness and wickedness" of humankind
1 Corinthians 6:9-11
A warning that "wrongdoers will not inherit the kingdom of God"
Ephesians 5:33
The ideal marriage relationship
Jude 7
A reference to Sodom and Gomorrah

The first thing one may observe about this list, which seems at an initial glance to be rather substantial, is what is *not* there: there is no record in the Bible that either Jesus or any of the Old Testament prophets ever made any reference at all to same-sex relations.

Turning now to the passages which do seem to refer to such relations, we saw in the previous chapter that the story of Sodom as recorded in Genesis 19 is primarily designed to emphasize the importance of hospitality. The same can be said of the gruesome account in Judges 19. It is an interesting reflection on the Bible's estimate of hospitality, in relation to its attitude towards sexual sin, that when Jericho was destroyed (Joshua 6), the only persons spared were the prostitute Rahab, who had shown hospitality to Joshua's spies, and her family.

The references cited from Deuteronomy and the two books of Kings all refer to temple prostitution, which was a feature of Canaanite religion against which the Israelites were warned again and again. These condemnations and prohibitions of both heterosexual and homosexual prostitution evidently have nothing to say about long-term relationships of any kind.

The creation story in Genesis 1 and the historically earlier one recorded in Genesis 2 both give accounts of the original relationship of Adam and Eve. Since according to these stories no other human beings existed at the time, they naturally make no reference to any other kind of relationship. It is noteworthy that in the older of the two accounts (Genesis 2) the relationship of Adam and Eve is portrayed in terms of being designed for their total companionship, whereas in the later story (Genesis 1) the purpose of their togetherness is described as multiplying and subduing the earth.

The verse cited from Ephesians 5 is concerned with both the affirmation of the relationship of Christ with his body the church and the relationship of husband and wife. The writer makes no mention here of any other kind of human relationship, and if the inference is drawn — as some have done from this text — that the husband-wife relationship is the only possible one for Christians, it would follow that the state of celibacy is also sinful.

The passage in Jude uses Sodom — as did all the major prophets and Jesus — as an illustration of the destruction that inevitably follows sinfulness. Unlike Jesus and the prophets, however, the writer does mention "unnatural sexual lusts" as one of the sins of Sodom. But as we have seen in the previous chapter, it requires a considerable level of pre-judgment to see this as a reference to what we now know as homosexual relationships.

This leaves the very important references in Leviticus, Romans and 1 Corinthians. All four clearly refer to sexual relations between people of the same gender and equally clearly condemn such activity. For many people who wish to hold to a high view of the Bible and its authority, these verses settle the matter. Multitudes of Christians, including many scholars, do exactly that: on the basis of these verses they argue that the Bible prohibits same-sex relations as evil, indeed, so serious an evil that Paul says quite categorically that people who do such things will not enter the kingdom of God.

But other Christians would insist that there are different ways to interpret these texts without abandoning the Bible's authority. The Leviticus texts appear in that section of Leviticus known as the Holiness Code, which sets out how the behaviour of the Israelites as God's chosen people was to be distinct from that of other nations. In that life of holiness homosexual relations between men were forbidden. The reason why women are not mentioned, students of the Old Testament suggest, is that it was believed at that time that the total source of a new life came from the man, with the woman serving only as the vessel in which the seed developed into a new life. In a small nation surrounded by powerful neighbours and longing to increase, any action in which the seeds of a possible new life were wasted was declared to be sinful.

But whether or not such a scientific misunderstanding lies behind this prohibition, there is a more serious problem with interpreting the Leviticus verses as a blanket condemnation, coming with the authority of the Bible, of any sexual relation-ship between two men. This is that even those who do so most firmly never seem to follow the same method of understanding when they read the neighbouring verses. Both among individual Christians who wish to take the Bible seriously and in the many churches that have cited the Leviticus prohibition in official reports as authoritative, it is usual to insist that people who do

42

behave in such a way must be treated with loving compassion and assisted in a process of change. But Leviticus says quite explicitly that those who engage in such activities must be executed. Other parts of the Holiness Code forbid a host of other things which, so far as I know, are not taken seriously by any modern Christians — for example, eating meat containing blood, wearing garments made of two types of fibre or appointing as priests someone with any physical defect, even a twisted eyebrow.

This inevitably raises the question: how is it possible to determine that one verse in this passage is to be taken as having divine authority while rejecting so many others alongside it as not applicable for us today? I do not know how to answer that question, and I have never received a satisfactory reply when I have asked those who do make such a determination. But many Christians whom I respect take this selective view of how the Holiness Code is to be interpreted. Their reasons for understanding it should thus be shared and tested in ecumenical discussions.

To consider, alternatively, that the Holiness Code and all its laws and prohibitions were determined by the cultural and religious stage at which the people of Israel were at the time it was written is not of course to say that none of the things in those chapters has any relevance or value to us in our time. But it is to say that the Code in its entirety is not to be granted absolute authority over us today just because it is recorded in the biblical book of Leviticus.

What then of Paul's injunctions in Romans and 1 Corinthians? These verses also refer quite explicitly to same-gender relations, and with the same abhorrence as the Leviticus passages. Moreover, alone of all biblical writers, Paul (though only once) refers to same-gender relations between women as well as between men. Once again there are many churches and individual Christians who want to see these verses as finally settling the issue with divine authority. But it is important to notice that in neither passage is Paul referring to those who would be described, according to our contemporary understanding, as being of homosexual orientation. He specifically refers to the fact that the persons in view here had been living in heterosexual relationships and had abandoned them in favour of homosexual relationships. This point must not be pressed too far, for while Paul knew that certain people engaged in such activities he had no concept of an orientation in that direction. Like everyone until fairly recently, he assumed that in every case it was just a matter of conscious choice and not in any case a matter of unchangeable orientation.

Gennaro Avvento observes that Paul's reference to same-gender sex in this passage is not singled out or highlighted in any way, but appears almost parenthetically in a list of sins resulting from idolatry.[1] And this in turn points to a problem similar to that mentioned in our discussion of Leviticus for those who want to see the words of Paul as an unquestioned and authoritative prohibition of all homosexual activity. In the passage in the letter to the Corinthians Paul declares that not only those who engage in same-gender relationships will be excluded from the kingdom of God, but also all thieves, greedy people, drunkards, slanderers and swindlers. It is my impression that those who regard Paul's words on same-gender relations here as having divine authority would not give similar status to the apparently unequivocal exclusion of the other groups from the kingdom of God.

The alternative to giving final authority to a particular literal reading of certain verses in Scripture and disregarding others from the same context is to accept the fact that the Bible is a very human book, written over a period of approximately twelve hundred years, written by some great — but no less human — persons who lived in a cultural situation radically different from ours. The written words speak to us today as we read them with the guidance of the Holy Spirit, and supremely through the life, teaching, death and resurrection of Jesus Christ. Admittedly, this means that the path of understanding is not always easy to find or to follow; at the same time, it does deliver us from an enslavement to selected verses chosen by someone else.

Examining these specific passages of Scripture which refer to same-gender sexual relationships, as we have done, is ultimately only one facet of a much wider question: can we find in the Bible a sexual ethic to guide us in handling the sexual dimension of our nature, whether heterosexual, homosexual or bisexual? The answer to that question is that we cannot and in fact do not. The Bible makes many references to sex, but it is not concerned with "sexuality" as such, and there is no word for that concept in either Old Testament Hebrew or New Testament Greek. Scripture is not a textbook on sexual ethics, and to attempt to derive such an ethical system from selected texts is to misuse the Bible. Jesus dealt with women and men on the same level, in a way which shocked his contemporaries, and his actions have ethical implications for us. But he made no attempt to teach a new sexual ethic.

Paul was writing to Christians in Corinth at a specific point in time when that city was notorious for vice of all kinds. The temple to Aphrodite there is reported to have been served by a thousand prostitutes. Around the Roman empire a common name for a prostitute was "a Corinthian girl". Paul does not condemn marriage nor sexual intimacy within it. In that regard he gave equal rights to husbands and wives. He believed that the end of the world was imminent and therefore recommended celibacy as the wiser course under the circumstances. But he did not seek to lay down a permanent or comprehensive sexual ethic.

Besides including a few texts which certainly condemn same-gender sexual relationships, the Bible also reflects other sexual norms and practices from ancient times which Christians and many others today would certainly reject. For example, in Old Testament times nudity was regarded as shameful (see, for example, Ezekiel 22:10). Consider what harm has been done in race relations as a consequence of the story of Noah's sons (Genesis 9:20-27). One of them — and the millions of his descendants ever since — have been regarded as inferior, discriminated against and oppressed, justified on the basis of the curse recorded here because that son looked on his father's nakedness whereas the other two walked into their father's tent backwards to cover him without seeing his naked body. Again, women were regarded as unclean for seven days after their menstrual period, and intercourse within that period was forbidden on pain of death. Most of the biblical laws concerning adultery and prostitution were established on the understanding that women were the property of men. A man using a prostitute was not guilty of sin, though the prostitute was. An unmarried man was not condemned for such action, but a woman discovered not to be a virgin at marriage was to be stoned to death. Owning female slaves, taking concubines and using women prisoners for sexual amusement was common in the culture reflected in the Old Testament. Polygamy was taken for granted and many of the figures portrayed most favourably in the Old Testament had more than one wife. Some scholars suggest that the New Testament instruction that bishops and deacons should have only one wife is not a prohibition of divorce and remarriage but a reference to the contemporary possibility of their having two wives at the same time.

David, the most honoured of kings, credited with writing some of the most wonderful psalms, had six sons by different women in the seven-and-a-half years he ruled from Hebron and twenty-one during the long period in which he ruled from Jerusalem, not to mention those born to his concubines. Except for Tamar, who appears in the sordid story of rape recorded in 2 Samuel 13, the daughters born to him are not mentioned, for they were clearly assumed to be of little or no importance. Whatever the injunctions of the Mosaic law, it was the conduct of leaders like David and Solomon which set the standard of acceptability.

It is often suggested that the laws and customs of the old covenant were abrogated by the new covenant in Jesus Christ. Virtually all Christians would agree that the provisions of this covenant dealing with the cultic life of the pre-Christian era were superseded, and most would say the same of much of the moral code that went along with it. Given the fact that nearly everyone in our time rejects the moral provisions of that code applying to the sexual relations between men and women, why nevertheless give authority to a single Old Testament statement regarding same-gender sexual relations among men? Some would reply that while Paul also rejected much from under the old covenant, he still reaffirmed the prohibition of same-gender sexual relationships. But do we properly understand Paul if we try to turn his words into a new and timeless law?

I have implied what my own interpretation of these verses is, but my purpose in this chapter and indeed in this book is not so much to advance a particular interpretation as to express the ecumenical need for a truly open conversation among those whose interpretations on these points differ. To me it seems evident that in nearly every respect our contemporary Christian understanding of sexual relationships stems not only or even primarily from our understanding of specific biblical verses, but also from many other factors, including much information not available to people in biblical times. Yet many debates in churches on matters relating to homosexuality seem to focus on the interpretation of certain texts from the Bible; and for that reason I have tried to suggest a responsible contemporary reading of these passages.

The texts we have considered in this chapter have been the ones used by the churches in their debate about and frequent condemnation of people engaged in same-gender sex. But it is important to note that restricting the discussion of the biblical testimony to these particular texts ignores that part of the scriptural message to which gay and lesbian people refer when they are speaking for themselves. The churches must also listen to their exposition of the biblical passages which guide their faith.

To quote from the biblical scholar Walter Wink:

> The fact is that there is, behind the legal tenor of scripture, an even deeper tenor, articulated by Israel out of the experience of the Exodus and brought to sublime embodiment in Jesus' identification with harlots, tax collectors, the diseased and maimed and outcast and poor. It is that God sides with the powerless, God liberates the oppressed. God suffers with the suffering and groans towards the reconciliation of all things. In the light of that supernal compassion, whatever our position on gays, the gospel's imperative to love, care for and be identified with their sufferings is unmistakably clear.[2]

That deeper sense of Scripture should, it would seem, exercise far greater authority than the more detailed references from Leviticus and the epistles of Paul, about whose interpretation, we have seen, a great deal of ambiguity has arisen.

NOTES

[1] *Sexuality: A Christian View*, Mystic, Connecticut, Twenty-Third Publications, 1982.
[2] "Biblical Perspectives on Homosexuality", *Christian Century*, vol. 96, no. 36, 7 Nov. 1979, p.1086.

6. The Shadow of History

The full story of the place of homosexual activity in the history of the human race will never be told, for much of it has been kept secret by the people who practised it and ignored or denied in cultures where it was never acknowledged or legally and religiously condemned. But in dealing with the related issues in our time, it is necessary to take careful notice of some of the important glimpses available to us from the past.

We have already said that homosexual relationships have existed in every human society of the past and the present, whatever the degree of repression or toleration at a particular time. There are references to it in the cuneiform script of clay tablets dating back to a period more than two thousand years before the birth of Christ. In Greek civilization and in the early centuries of the Roman empire, same-sex activity, especially among the rich and powerful and between owners and slaves, was taken for granted.

Classical Greece accepted love-making between men to a degree never known since. This is clearly reflected in much Greek love poetry. It was very common, for example, for two women or two men to be recognized as lovers without involving legal issues of property. Aristotle described with approval some male lovers who spent their whole lives together and wanted to be buried together. There are many references in literature to the Sacred Band of Thebes, made up of homosexual lovers fighting side by side. It was evident that (contrary to the conventional military wisdom today) their love for one another made them braver and more loyal to one another, and for a long period the Sacred Band was regarded as invincible. Many Greek writers, far from regarding participation in same-sex relationships as effeminate, declared that such love was found in the bravest and most manly nations (and they would have been shocked at the modern inclusion of women in military forces). They also believed that same-sex relationships were inherently far more stable than heterosexual relationships.

In Roman times, Julius Caesar was described as "every woman's man, and every man's woman". Nero was twice publicly married to other men. For at least 200 years after the Roman empire became officially Christian, male prostitution was taxed — which certainly implies that it was at least officially tolerated. Indeed, there was very little intolerance of

48

homosexual relationships in the Roman era, and they were not illegal under Roman law until the third century, and then it was only male marriages and the abuse of minors which were forbidden. Homosexual actions as such became illegal only in the sixth century. The suggestion sometimes made that homosexual relationships contributed to the downfall of the empire is a misreading of history: such relationships were most tolerated when the empire was at its height, and it was in the centuries of its decline that intolerance appeared.

But the main focus of our interest in the past in this book is on the development of the Judaeo-Christian tradition. As noted earlier, the Hebrew repugnance towards nakedness, patriarchal treatment of women, strict national exclusivism and rejection of the prostitution practices of Canaanite religion all became incorporated into the Christian heritage. The association of homosexual activity with heresy and unfaithfulness towards God persisted through the Middle Ages and was often used to justify bloody persecutions. Despite the humanitarian ideals of many Christians, the churches throughout their history have remained the most powerful official pressure groups opposing sexual freedom in such areas as birth control, abortion, divorce, premarital intercourse and homosexual relationships.

For nearly three thousand years the Judaeo-Christian tradition articulated its sexual morality largely in terms of the link between intercourse and procreation, in the process becoming far more repressive than is justifiable on the basis of the Bible. The tradition was much influenced by the Talmud, written at the time of the early Christians, and by the strong reaction of the early church fathers to the licentiousness of their Graeco-Roman environment. It is interesting that the universal use of the Sodom story in early Christian times was not based on the interpretation of this story throughout Scripture, as we saw in an earlier chapter, but on the version made popular by Philo of Alexandria (ca. 13 B.C.E.-50 C.E.): namely, that the city was destroyed for same-gender sexual activity. This misinterpreted story had a far more profound effect on the early fathers of the church than any of the teaching in Leviticus or Paul's epistles, and that influence continues down to modern times, not only on Christian ethical teaching but also on state laws since the codes of Justinian and Theodosius.

During the difficult early centuries of the Christian movement, its outstanding leaders and theologians expressed very extreme views about sexuality. Sex was regarded by Augustine as an "unfortunate necessity" for procreation. Origen and Jerome considered all sexual pleasure as evil. Jerome is quoted, perhaps mistakenly, as saying that "a man who loves his wife too much is an adulterer. An upright man should love his wife with his judgment, not with his affections." Augustine wrote that "there is nothing which degrades a manly spirit more than the attraction of females and contact with their bodies". At the same time, the Jewish rabbinical law condemned anal intercourse and prescribed death by stoning as punishment. Such views of sexuality were obviously influential in creating the hermit movement and ultimately the celibate monastic orders. In the fourth century some states under the influence of the church tradition prescribed mutilation, hanging or deportation as punishment for homosexual activities. Partly due also to the church fathers, laws condemning homosexual relations, primarily buggery, were increasingly imposed after the time of Constantine, until in the sixth century the punishment was burning at the stake (the origin of the slang term "faggots" for homosexual people). Within the church some penitentials prescribed punishments even for males kissing one another.

St Thomas Aquinas and scholastic theology ranked — in ascending order of seriousness — masturbation, sodomy and bestiality as sins "against nature". By this emphasis the Leviticus prohibition became not only the accepted ethical norm but part of the Western criminal code. Vast numbers of people were tortured and exterminated by the Inquisition for same-gender relationships. In France such persons continued to be burned alive until the eighteenth century; in England the death penalty for practising homosexuals remained in force until 1861, when it was replaced by life imprisonment.

On the other hand, the church of the Middle Ages can be seen as officially somewhat reticent on the subject of sex. While the legal status of homosexual persons was questioned in the fourth and fifth centuries, it was not denied until the sixth century. Gay marriages were legally permitted in the Roman empire until the year 342, and forcing males into prostitution was made a capital offence only in 390. When in 533 the first laws were enacted in any part of the empire making homosexual actions a capital offence, two bishops were among those immediately punished. It is quite clear that while the vigorous condemnation of sexual pleasure by the church fathers eventually had great influence on both church and state, it took a long time to achieve, and did not determine human activity to any great degree. It is also noteworthy that those same church fathers also condemned lending money at interest, sexual contact with a woman during menstruation, jewellery of all kinds, dyed fabrics, shaving, regular bathing, the use of wigs, serving in the government or the army and all manual labour on feast days. The first general church council to deal explicitly with homosexual activity was the Third Lateran Council in 1179.

Significant new insight into the inconsistency within the Christian tradition between theological teaching and practice is set forth in John Boswell's recent book *Same Sex Unions in Pre-Modern Europe*, which traces the development of Christian liturgies for uniting two people of the same sex.[1] Prior to the year 1000, Boswell says, marriages of lay people were consecrated by the church only as a favour, and non-consecration by the church did not invalidate a marriage. Tertullian, Cyril of Alexandria and Augustine refer only to the blessing of the bride prior to the marriage; and nuptial blessing was required only for priests. Not until the Fourth Lateran Council (1215) was marriage declared a sacrament:

> The earliest Greek liturgical manuscript, probably written in the eighth century in Italy…, contains four ceremonies for sacramental union. One was for heterosexual betrothal, two separate ceremonies for heterosexual marriage and a comparable prayer for uniting two men. There are many similarities of wording between the heterosexual union ceremony and the ceremony for same-sex union…
>
> There are at least seven other known versions of such a ceremony before the twelfth century and 17 surviving from the twelfth century itself written in Greek and Old Slavonic. The ceremony occurs in manuscripts from all over the known world.

The ceremony involved burning candles, placing the hands of the two parties on the gospel, joining their right hands, binding their hands with the priest's stole, reciting the Lord's prayer and partaking of communion; after which each participant would kiss the gospel, the priest and the other participant. No matter how this service was officially described, it would certainly be seen as a marriage by the participants and their families. Boswell continues:

> In fact sustained and effective oppression of those engaged in homosexual behaviour was not known in Europe until the thirteenth century, and was never common in the Byzantine East. Penalties against lesbian activities, though very rare, appear to have been aimed exclusively at nuns and they were surprisingly mild.

As homosexual relations came to be legally and socially regarded with increasing distaste from the twelfth century on, there was little impetus for maintaining the use of a religious rite establishing same-sex personal relationships. It was equally inevitable that considerable effort would go into downgrading the meaning of the rite, especially by describing it as the creation of a bond of friendship, despite the fact that it always involved only two people and never more.

Between the mid-eleventh and mid-twelfth centuries there was another short period when homosexual relationships had relatively wide acceptance, and many signs appeared in literature and in European society of what could be described as a gay culture. But this was followed by a period of rapidly rising intolerance in sexual matters. In 1179 the Third Lateran Council condemned homosexual people — along with money-lenders, heretics, Jews, Muslims and mercenaries. In the thirteenth century any Christian having intercourse with a Jewish person was condemned as having intercourse with an animal. This was the age of the Crusades, and it was a time when the most intimate activities of married couples were subject to rigid criticism. Coitus interruptus, oral intercourse, anal intercourse, indeed, any departure from the male dominating position in intercourse were declared to be "against nature". Any expression of sexual feelings was denied to children, handicapped people, unmarried and celibate persons, divorced or widowed people, because sexual contact of any kind was assumed to be related only to procreation (although the marriage of people over child-bearing age continued to be allowed).

Such repressive attitudes to sexuality have persisted in many places to the present time, and are widely identified with the

Western Judaeo-Christian tradition, which has also dominated the countries of the third world wherever there is a history of Western colonial and missionary expansion. The widespread ignorance which such a religiously and legally repressive environment fosters offers fertile soil for the flourishing of erroneous myths and stereotypes. This explains the prevalence in most Western and Western-influenced countries of the assumptions that homosexual men are always effeminate and homosexual women always masculine, that all homosexual people are promiscuous, that male homosexual activity consists exclusively of anal intercourse and that abuse of minors is predominantly carried out by gay men. All researchers declare emphatically that while these characteristics and behaviours might be true of individual homosexuals, they are totally false as generalizations. As is always the case with stereotypes, the result of such ignorant and unfounded prejudices is inevitably the inflicting of injustice and suffering on certain human beings.

Historically, while lesbian relationships were condemned morally and in some cases made illegal, they were treated with considerably more tolerance than relationships among gay men. Apart from references to cultic prostitution, the Bible contains only one mention of female homosexual relationships. A number of reasons may be suggested for this. In the Hebrew understanding the male partner alone provided the seed of a new life, so the focus of concern was on male activity. The emotional revulsion at anal intercourse which reinforced the condemnation of sexual relationships between men could not apply to women. It is also assumed that the sexually motivated contacts in many lesbian relationships were satisfying without advancing to genital actions.

On the other hand, double standards of morality — one for men, one for women — are found in both the Hebrew and Christian environments. In Old Testament times it was not regarded as a sin for a man to use the services of a prostitute, but she was considered a sinner. A bride found not to be a virgin was condemned to death in a way certainly not applicable to men who had previously been promiscuous. Many aspects of this double standard persist in popular ethical understanding to this day.

Even this brief overview of the past treatment of people engaged in same-gender sexual relationships is sufficient to indicate the radical change in understanding that results when it is recognized that for some people the desire for such relationships is innate and unchangeable, and in no way an act of choice for which they can be held responsible. In earlier centuries, people were unaware of that fact. As we look back over long periods of cruelty towards homosexual people, we may qualify our condemnations of such treatments in view of the degree of their ignorance. But those who continue to call for such harsh attitudes today, given the greater understanding we have available, are in urgent need of repentance and of the changes of attitude and behaviour which repentance involves.

NOTE

[1] New York, Villard Press, 1994.

7. The Winds of Change

There is much evidence in this century of changing attitudes towards homosexually oriented people. This is the case in scientific circles, in governments and in churches, but it is far from universal.

The modern scientific recognition that sexual orientation in most cases is not something chosen creates a radical revolution in any responsible estimate of homosexual people. Researchers increasingly agree that while some persons have a flexible orientation, which can therefore be influenced one way or another, the majority of people are heterosexually oriented and a small but significant minority are homosexually oriented.

The growing rejection of the traditional myths that have caused so much misunderstanding and abuse of homosexual people — although these myths persist in many places, including many churches — is reflected in shifting public attitudes. In many places this greater public openness is evident in literature, films, theatre and television programmes, as well as in a range of areas of everyday life. For example, in Britain the "Play Index" for 1968-72 listed 28 plays under the heading "homosexual" and five others under the heading "lesbian". Many of these have been made into films. Homophile clubs are now routinely listed among the activities available for students at most British universities.

At the political level, too, change is coming about, even if it is often slow, and many governments at all levels continue to try to legislate homosexual activity out of existence. Approximately 3000 military personnel in the US are discharged every year for engaging in homosexual activities, and a commitment by President Bill Clinton, shortly after his inauguration in 1993, to remove long-standing prohibitions on gay and lesbian people in the armed forces touched off a bitter and politically damaging controversy in many circles in the US. But a growing number of governments are decriminalizing homosexual relations under specified conditions.[1] When the former German Democratic Republic legalized homosexual relations in 1968, the age of consent for both heterosexual and homosexual people was set at 16 years. In 1969 West Germany made gay relationships legal at the age of 18, although the age of consent for heterosexual people remained at 14.

In some areas, provisions have been established which allow for the legal registration of homosexual partnerships. In Denmark, where such a law went into effect in October 1989, more than 800 such couples were registered in three years. While the provisions for ending these relationships were similar to Danish divorce laws for heterosexual couples, only seven homosexual couples requested legal termination of their relationship in the first two years after the law went into effect. Similar laws were enacted in Norway in 1993 and in Sweden in 1994. A matter of considerable controversy in certain jurisdictions where laws of this type have been passed is whether such couples should be permitted to adopt children.

Churches in Britain, Australia, the United States and Aotearoa New Zealand have made significant contributions to moves by governments in these countries to decriminalize homosexual relationships and to enact laws preventing discrimination against homosexual persons in matters of employment and accommodation. At the same time, in all the countries listed, many people in the churches exerted pressure against such political changes.

But even church groups that maintain the tradition that homosexual acts are sinful have affirmed the non-sinfulness of homosexual orientation as such. These include Roman Catholic and evangelical Protestant groups. While they could not speak officially for their churches, working parties appointed by the Roman Catholic, Anglican and Methodist Churches in Britain have all accepted homosexual activity within certain limits for those whose orientation is unchangeable.

We have seen that many biblical scholars now express the view that the same-gender sexual relationships portrayed and condemned in the Bible are irrelevant to our modern understanding of homosexual orientation. Some interpret the biblical and modern understandings of homosexual relations in such a way as to affirm that loving, long-term committed homosexual relationships are not condemned in Scripture at all. That statement is endorsed, for example, by the Christian Association for Psychological Studies in the United States.

The number of Christian and church-related organizations providing fellowship for homosexual Christians and advocating for changes in attitudes, church regulations and laws regarding homosexuality has grown rapidly in recent years. Among the best-known are the Open Church Group, the Gay Christian Movement, the Roman Catholic group Quest and Friends Homosexual Fellowship. In the United States the Metropolitan Community Church, formed by gay and lesbian persons who have felt unable for a variety of reasons to remain within the Christian denominations of which they were members, brings together a large number of congregations. Its existence and status as a church have created considerable ecumenical con- troversy in other US churches. Already in 1963 the Quakers published "Towards a Quaker View of Sex", which argued that homosexual relationships can be as permanent and selfless as heterosexual ones. Love can be sincere in either type of relation- ship or betrayed in either type.

A semi-official document by some Roman Catholic bishops in the USA in 1973 fully accepted the fact that homosexual people do not choose their orientation. It advised priests to clear their own minds of the myths about homosexual people and not to recommend them for psychoanalytic treatment. On the other hand, the document retained the long-standing Catholic view that homosexual acts are a grave transgression and that genital relations are allowable only within marriage. Biblical teaching was accepted as final condemnation of homosexual activity, though it is noteworthy that the document refrained from using the Sodom story in support of that position.

A 1978 British publication entitled "Towards a Charter of Homosexual Rights" included among its 175 sponsors some 45 clergy. That publication likened fear of homosexual people to the injustice of racism. It pointed out that heterosexually oriented people may also have a dark side but that nobody questions the right to marry because of the existence of prostitu- tion and rape.

A significant example of this changing situation occurred in Britain in March 1995. Derek Rawcliffe, the former Anglican bishop of Glasgow and Galloway, announced that he was homosexual and called for a church blessing on gay couples. The announcement came a day after Cardinal Basil Hume, leader of the Roman Catholic Church in England and Wales, condemned homophobia and discrimination against homosexuals. While reaffirming his support for the Vatican statement that homosexual genital acts are "objectively disordered" and "morally wrong", Cardinal Hume declared that it "is a fundamental human right of every person, irrespective of sexual orientation, to be treated by individuals and by society with dignity, respect and fairness" and that the church "has a duty to oppose discrimination in all circumstances where a person's sexual orientation or activity cannot reasonably be regarded as relevant".[2]

Rawcliffe's call for a church blessing reflects a growing debate within many churches about whether homosexual couples who wish to make a long-term commitment of faithfulness to one another should be able to do so publicly within the context of the church. As one writer has expressed it, "If we can bless battleships, we can surely bless two men or two women who want to make solemn vows of faithfulness to one another." While most churches have been determined to preserve the absolute uniqueness of heterosexual marriage services, many clergy are in fact quietly performing such services of blessing.

Even in churches which regard the biblical prohibitions of same-gender sexual relationships as having final authority, many are nevertheless working to overcome the homophobia which has bedevilled the pastoral responsibility of the church. Their attribution of divine authority to two verses in Leviticus while ignoring related verses demanding the death penalty for homosexual acts may be inconsistent, but at least this inconsistency allows them to promote compassion and openness in pastoral dialogue with homosexually oriented people and to reject myths which have done such injustice.

It is impossible within the scope of this short book — nor is it our purpose — to summarize in detail the present state of the overall human understanding of and dealing with people of homosexual orientation. On the one hand, we will not find many people agreeing with the remark attributed to the ancient Greek philosopher Epicurus that "nobody was ever the better for the carnal act, and a man may be thankful if he is not definitely the worse". Yet the hostile pressures persist. In my own country more gay men die of suicide than of AIDS. The variety of strongly held opinions remains. For some, whatever may be said of homosexual orientation, any genital acts expressing that orientation are intrinsically evil. The only acceptable Christian life-style for such people on this understanding is celibacy. Others are more tolerant but still regard same-gender relations as essentially imperfect. Yet others express their judgment only on the quality of the love relationship, whether it be a heterosexual or homosexual couple involved. And finally there are those who simply accept that some people are created unchangeably homosexual and for them same-gender relationships are inevitable and normal.

To approach this issue from the perspective of the Christian church is to raise dimensions of the question which are both more profound and more intensely practical. What is at stake is not only the way Scripture is to be interpreted, but also the very nature of the church itself. These form the theological background to a debate which is focussed on yet another basic concern for all Christians, a deep question of justice being done in Christ's name. This debate cannot be confined to the theological classroom, since the real-life situation faces churches with questions that demand administrative and policy answers.

These questions can be summarized as follows.
1. Is it recognized that in every community and every church there is an important minority of people with an unchangeable homosexual orientation?
2. Is such orientation a barrier to the admission of a gay man or lesbian woman into (a) full membership and (b) positions of leadership within the church?
3. Are the same answers given to the above questions if the gay man or lesbian woman is openly living in a same-gender relationship of committed permanence?
4. Will the church give some recognition or blessing to such a relationship if it is mature and committed to long-term faithfulness?

It is important to recognize that these questions are not directed to the homosexual minority of church members, but to the heterosexual majority who make the decisions. It may be that the Spirit of Jesus Christ is leading us into new truth and greater love in this age. He is certainly calling us ecumenically to seek the truth together.

NOTES

[1] In the draft of a paper entitled "Getting Lesbian and Gay Issues on the International Human Rights Agenda" (to be published in a forthcoming issue of *Human Rights Quarterly*), Douglas Sanders of the faculty of law in the University of British Columbia provides this list of the growing number of states that have now decriminalized homosexual activity:
1961: Illinois, Hungary, Czechoslovakia
1967: England and Wales
1968: Bulgaria, German Democratic Republic
1969: Canada, Federal Republic of Germany
1971: Finland, Austria
1972: Norway, South Australia
1973: Malta
1976: Australian Capital Territory
1977: Four republics and autonomous provinces in Yugoslavia (Slovenia, Voivodina, Croatia and Montenegro)
1980: Scotland, Victoria (Australia)
1982: Northern Ireland
1983: Australian Northern Territory, Guernsey
1984: Cuba, New South Wales
1986: Aotearoa New Zealand
1989: Western Australia, Liechtenstein
1990: Queensland, Jersey
1991: Ukraine, Hong Kong
1992: Latvia, Estonia, Gibraltar, Isle of Man
1993: Russian Federation, Lithuania, Ireland, Kazakhstan
1994: Serbia, Bermuda
1995: Albania, Cyprus, Moldova
    There are still criminal prohibitions of homosexual activity in about half the states in the US and in Tasmania. These actions of decriminalization clear the way for anti-discrimination regulations.
[2] *Ecumenical News International Bulletin*, 95-0071, 14 March 1995, p.3.

Appendix:
Three Personal Stories

The following texts are included here primarily to provide "real life" examples of people of homosexual orientation, and of how they have dealt with their situations. This is a further illustration of the view already expressed: that as Christians our discussion of issues related to homosexuality can be effective only if we are thinking in terms of actual people, and not just in terms of culturally inherited ideas and prejudices.

A Family Story
GAE AND JOLEEN CHERRY

I wish to thank my family, Neil, Jo and Karla, for their openness, honesty and willingness to share a very private part of our lives.

Neil and I met as students at a Baptist youth group in 1965. We had both been brought up in conservative Christian communities. While Neil had a questioning approach, my background led me to accept the traditional Christian values of my parents, who were leaders in our local Baptist church.

My deep interest in children led me into teaching, specializing in education of the deaf. This brought me to Christchurch in 1965, where I met Neil, who was studying physics at the university.

During our three years of courtship we were part of an intellectually stimulating church group, studying the latest theology. I began to question many of the conservative Baptist teachings I had previously considered as absolutes, though both of us retained very traditional moral and ethical values, including no alcohol, drugs or intercourse before marriage. In preparation for our marriage we read many books, attended courses and discussed every topic under the sun. We shared a deep concern for peace and justice, participated in the first anti-nuclear demonstrations and supported the anti-apartheid movement.

Our personal theological journeys brought us both to the point where we rejected our childhood images of God. For us, God is not external and male, but is the source of life and love in all of us.

As Christians we hold that all people are made in God's image. We see all people as "whole people". Jesus clearly saw beyond external appearances to the person. People felt and knew Jesus' love and acceptance, whether they were old or young, lame or able-bodied, male or female. We have found that it is more creative and loving to celebrate our differences and to discover the rich and diverse contributions each of us can make to our relationships and to our society.

Neil and I were married in 1968. I continued teaching deaf children and Neil undertook doctoral research. In 1971 Joleen was born. Soon afterwards our new family moved to Montreal, where we took part in a wide diversity of activities and encountered a wide variety of attitudes. We were active in an interesting Presbyterian congregtion which was attempting to provide a supportive community in the inner city.

After we moved back to Aotearoa New Zealand, Karla was born in 1974. To give our daughters a rich and varied childhood it was very important for me to be with them in their formative years. I became involved in their pre-school, a family cooperative play-centre, and extended my training to include child development and parent education at the pre-school level.

As a pre-schooler Joleen quickly became a leader of boisterous activity, leading a group of children in adventurous play. I did not realize that the boys didn't know Joleen was a girl until one day she wore a dress and they asked me who this new girl was. At first, they rejected her, but when they discovered that their games were not the same without her, they let her back into their inner circle. This shows how early stereotyping and prejudice can start.

From age three Jo expressed the wish that she had been born a boy. When asked why, she said she "wanted to be rough and tough" and "only boys do exciting things". We spent a lot of time showing her that she could be whoever she wanted to be. We discovered that none of the books we were reading had as a main character a girl doing adventurous activities. An extensive search of bookshops failed to locate even one such book.

Karla was the opposite from Jo in many ways. While encouraging each of the girls in their chosen activities, we also tried to broaden their interests in other areas to make them more well-rounded people. Since we felt that our local state school was encouraging stereotypes and focussing too much on the academic at the expense of the creative sides of our girls, we made a decision which for us at the time was very radical: to send Jo, and later Karla, to the Rudolf Steiner School, as this offered development of the creative and academic sides of Jo's interests, the freedom she craved to wear what she was comfortable in, to play how she liked.

Neil was lecturing at university and spent as much time as he could with our daughters, helping them to build tree huts, ride bicycles and learn about the natural world, while I enjoyed planning creative activities, encouraging drama and music, and allowing lots of messes in the house and kitchen as they learned new skills.

The culture in our family has always been tolerant and loving to all people. Having long worked with children who have disabilities, I have seen how difficult it can be to be different. Whenever we saw any kind of injustice we pointed it out to our daughters and tried to think of solutions. They both have well-developed social consciences.

I was also involved in the women's movement of the 1970s and really loved the atmosphere and ideas that came from the movement. Neil was never threatened by this and agreed that there were many injustices facing women in the world. During these years I met lesbian women for the first time. After initially feeling uncomfortable, I developed an understanding and acceptance of them as women like me whose only difference was their sexual orientation.

We were fortunate to spend a year in the United States in 1980-81. This gave Jo and Karla a totally different educational experience; and our family found an amazing United Church of Christ congregation which was non-judgmental and inclusive of a very diverse group of people who did not necessarily think alike but respected the views of others.

Returning to Aotearoa New Zealand I took up a new job as an early intervention therapist working with children who had multiple disabilities. Our articulate and challenging daughters were now attending the local state high school. As they grew older the challenges became more difficult. These teenage years were not easy, and at times I did not feel adequate for the task of bringing up two daughters who seemed bent on breaking all the rules and finding their own space in life. The knowledge that these years are important in throwing off the strictures of home and rebelling against the values of their parents kept us going when the going got tough. Supportive friends and relatives helped us through these tough times.

Having been reared in families with fairly traditional Christian values, Neil and I, like many other parents, tried to instill our value systems into our children. I found it easy to talk to the girls about sexual matters and I hoped they would not become sexually active early.

Jo got on best with boys as companions for sport and music rather than as "boy friends". On the other hand, she seemed to have strong friendships with her girl friends. I knew that it was not unusual for girls of her age to experience emotional attachments to other girls.

As she became older I began to suspect that she might be lesbian. Neil and I talked about it and wondered if "it was just a phase" or something more fundamental. We felt that the best thing we could do for her was to make the climate in our home such that any "coming out" would not be traumatic. This is not to say there was no sadness on our part initially, for we thought her life would be more difficult for her and us if she was lesbian. I suggested to her that she remain open to the possibility of having heterosexual relationships in the future.

Jo remembers that when she was at high school and went to the movies with girl friends, she found the female stars attractive while her friends were attracted to the male stars. She also identified in books and on television with the female characters. Realizing that this was a different response from that of her friends and that she had same-sex attractions, Jo went to the library to learn more about how the rest of the world viewed homosexuality. What she found were books describing homosexuality as sexual deviancy, dysfunction and abnormality. She was disappointed by this because she was comfortable with the way she felt. Her "logic of fairness" told her that it is not right to treat some differences in one way and other differences in another.

During the mid-1980s, parliamentary consideration of legislation to decriminalize homosexuality was widely discussed in the country, and nightly on television and daily in the newspapers Jo was seeing and hearing debates about homosexuality. For the first time she heard such derogatory terms as "faggot", "dyke", "poofter", "queer". And most of the opposition to the legislation was coming from certain Christian churches and organizations.

Jo could not understand how people who were supposed to be at the forefront of caring and compassion could talk about people like her as "an abomination", when she was just an ordinary woman who was attracted to women and not men. When trying to argue with people, she felt their arguments were illogical, but it frightened her to acknowledge her homosexuality in the high school setting because of the strongly emotive negative feelings being expressed by some teachers and fellow pupils.

As a high school student Jo was valued and liked for her skills in cricket and music, her friendliness and her sense of humour. She was perplexed and worried that she could well lose all of this if she "came out".

During our next visit to the United States (1986-87) Jo had a lovely relationship with a boy of 15, which I expected to turn into a "first love". He was a delightful young man and they got on very well, but I noticed that neither he nor Jo wanted any more than friendship. Her reaction was different from what I remembered of my own feelings at 15.

In her social group at school Jo saw that a boyfriend was a passport to being accepted and that the girls who didn't have boy friends never went anywhere socially. She made friends with several boys, which gave her not only access to the social scene but also gave her some good companions and friends who were boys.

Jo has had many friends, male and female, meeting them openly and warmly at an intellectual level, sharing ideas, music, humour and activities. She also found that young gay men and women often get on well together and form safe, non-sexual but socially acceptable relationships which ease their passage through the turbulent teenage years.

Jo's first big "crush" on a girl came when she was 16. This girl had a boy friend, and Jo dated his best friend for several months in order to spend time with her girl friend. But when Jo told her girl friend of her feelings for her, the girl obviously felt very uncomfortable with this declaration, and from this point they drifted apart. Years later they resumed contact and their earlier differences have been forgotten.

Soon after this, word spread around the school that Jo was probably a lesbian even though she had not made the decision to "come out". Derogatory comments were often directed at Karla, who was at the same high school, both about her sister and about her own sexuality. In retrospect, she recalls this as a difficult time, but by standing up for what she believed was fair and reasonable, she gained a great deal of personal strength and character.

At about 17, Jo often invited a girl friend to spend the night at our home. I knew this was an important part of socializing, but I suspected that a sexual relationship was beginning. As I recall, I asked her on one occasion, "Is there something you need to tell me about your relationship with — ?" Jo replied that she was having a relationship with her and that she thought she was lesbian. On reflection Jo does not remember this as a traumatic experience. She does recall that when she was about 13, she had asked me, "How would you feel if I was lesbian?" (probably during a general discussion about homosexuality), and my making an accepting response.

This put us in a quandary. We would certainly not have allowed her to have a boy in her bedroom overnight, but what about a girl? We felt that we could not say she could not have her girl friend around for the night, and that we needed to provide a safe place for them to explore their relationship, as it was not safe in the outside world to show affection for one another.

Within our family we talked openly about sexuality in general and how important it was to respect oneself and the other person. Becoming sexually active was a serious decision to make for many important reasons.

Discovering for the first time that one's children are sexually active is difficult for most parents. We found it just as difficult when Karla told us she was having a heterosexual relationship at 17 as when Jo told us about her homosexual relationship at a similar age. In fact, we were more concerned in Karla's case because of the possibility of sexually transmitted diseases and pregnancy (we recognize now, as we did not then, that all people need to practise safe sex, and that lesbians can also contract sexually transmitted diseases). As Karla made friendships with boys she objected to our not allowing her to have a boy stay overnight when we had allowed Jo to have her girl friend stay. How difficult parenting can be at these times!

I think most parents envisage a heterosexual future for their offspring and have dreams about who they may be and what they may do. It is important to put these dreams into perspective and vital to accept our children for who they are, not what we envisaged for them. This takes time and can be painful for both children and parents.

Jo has had three more relationships and has encountered considerable problems, including rejection by the parents of one of her girl friends and one unhappy abusive relationship. She has also had many positive and affirming experiences and has matured into an articulate, caring young woman. She has been in a committed and loving relationship with Mary since 1991.

Jo feels much safer since the law reform was passed, making it illegal to discriminate on the grounds of sexual orientation in employment, accommodation and the provision of goods and services. However there is still widespread prejudice and hostility directed at Jo and people she knows and loves.

Since leaving school and starting work, Karla has also enjoyed and appreciated her many friends in the gay community. She feels comfortable in a diverse downtown neighbourhood and believes her life would be much poorer without her gay friends.

We sometimes disagree with decisions made by each of our daughters, but we try to accept that the decisions are theirs. We enjoy an adult relationship with them which continues to improve, and we appreciate sharing their lives.

Our initial worries about other people's reactions to Jo's "coming out" as a lesbian were unfounded. Jo's decision not to worry about what other people think has enabled us to be completely open and matter-of-fact about our lesbian daughter and our support of gay people. We have found that the most common reaction from friends and colleagues to this openness is also matter-of-fact acceptance. Many have said that it has helped them come to terms with an issue which was difficult as an idea and that their perception of homosexuality has changed with real people involved. Some parents in similar situations have been helped through difficulties by our open and frank discussion of our family's journey and attitudes.

Some people take the position that they love and accept homosexual people but homosexual intimacy is a sin. Therefore, they say that homosexual people should be celibate. We believe that sexual intimacy is an integral part of our human experience, and that no person has the right to deny this to another. Celibacy is appropriate if chosen by the person, whether homosexual or heterosexual.

The failure to accept and love homosexual people as they are has tragic consequences. For example, on the basis of our daughters' experience we would suggest that an unknown and probably significant proportion of Aotearoa New Zealand's very high youth suicide rate is accounted for by homosexual young people who are too afraid to "come out" for fear of rejection and exclusion from their families.

What I have written here is about the philosophies and experiences of the members of my family. While each person and family is unique, the principles and philosophies we have developed, based deeply in our Christian faith and our image of God and Jesus, convince us that we as parents have made choices which have enriched and strengthened the life of our family and the lives of all its members, with all of our differences. This stands in contrast to families which are torn apart by the inability of some to accept the differences, including sexual orientation, of other family members.

We believe that the problems and solutions lie primarily with choices made by the parents and other family members. If you choose to regard homosexuality as an "abomination", a "mortal sin" or a curable disease, you are choosing a painful and destructive pathway for the family and the homosexual member. If you choose to accept and celebrate the rich diversity of attitudes, talents, contributions and sexual orientation of each family member, this can lead to a positive enrichment of every family member, a strengthening of the fabric of the family and an extension of the family's love and acceptance to others who have been excluded from theirs.

For us, this is the way of Jesus. We cannot conceive of Jesus turning his face away from either of our daughters, nor any person we know. Rather, we see Jesus greeting everyone with open arms and direct eye contact which communicates his love and acceptance to all. We can only strive to do likewise.

* * *

The following is a personal message from Jo:

I am a lesbian. I am also a musician, friend, sportsperson, cook, housekeeper and human being. Most of these attributes have not been a source of irritation or outright scorn from other people. For some illogical reason my sexual orientation is the focus of many people's attention, over and above all the other parts of my personality that make me who I am.

I was brought up in a white, middle-class, two-parent, one-sibling family in the affluent, predominantly Christian country of New Zealand. With all the privilege of my upbringing, I did not lack opportunities in my childhood. But all of the opportunities in the world did not shield me from the realities of life.

I choose to call myself "queer", as this term for me encompasses gay men, lesbians, transsexual and bisexual people. This word has been used as a derogatory term, but I choose to reclaim it as an inclusive term for those of us who have a different sexual orientation from heterosexual people. I am proud to be a part of this group of people who are struggling to educate ignorant and intolerant people that being "queer" is not bad, sick or sinful.

But in spite of the fact that a vast majority of us lead perfectly acceptable and, dare I say, normal lives, there is still a section of the society that abuses us through the media, in our work places and in our communities.

It is confusing and ridiculous that much of this abuse comes from Christian organizations and churches. I was brought up by Christian parents and I attended a Presbyterian church until the age of 15. I am not a Christian nor do I belong to any religious organization or group. I do not understand how people calling themselves Christians can preach love and forgiveness to some and hate and damnation to others.

Then there are the people that profess to support the gay, lesbian, transsexual and bisexual community, but still continue to perpetuate myths by believing that life would be easier for us if we had been heterosexual. Life would most certainly be easier for us if bigotry from some heterosexuals ceased. It is rude and insulting to be told by these "accepting people" that to make my life easier it is I, not they, who must change.

I decided about four years ago that I would not allow myself to repress my sexual orientation to save the embarrassment of other people who do not accept people as they are. I have made the very personal decision to be open about my homosexuality in a non-confrontational manner in every social situation. It would be nice not to have to do this, but it appears to be the only way to stop being presumed heterosexual. The process of "coming out" is a highly personal one and it is a violation of an individual's privacy to "out" another person without his or her permission.

There is a lot more to being lesbian than just the fact that I have a sexual relationship with another woman. We share a partnership that is filled with love, fun and commitment. In my opinion, this is the kind of relationship that the church could and should support.

I hope that this will happen in my lifetime.

An End to Silence

CLIVE PEARSON

Over an extended period of time I was given a rare privilege. A gay student of theology allowed me to "eavesdrop" on his experience. I had no intention other than to be available, to hear, to suggest how hints of a more personal theology might be drawn out — for there are no courses on gay or lesbian theology in the academy.

At one level, I saw these conversations as part of my job. I was also convinced that gay and lesbian theological voices need to be encouraged and released. So often the debate in the church is one in which gays become "them" rather than creative participants. So often the debate in the church is like an extended pastoral discussion, and the gay theological voice is not heard, because time, space and resources have not been set aside for this. There has been a lack of will, which leads to silence and silencing.

At a second level I wanted to hear how Christ might speak to me and address me through the experience of the "other". I was not disappointed. Let me share with you some of the things that came to the surface.

One of the first things we spoke about was how his understanding of a "calling" in Christ was tied to his "coming out" as gay. The theological significance of this should not be underestimated, for if this calling is indeed a genuine vocation, then we have a Christ who takes the initiative and bursts through the legal prescriptions which the church as an institution constructs. It means, of course, that the church, a "called community", is itself being addressed.

As a result of his theological education, this student experienced a rediscovery of liturgy and Scripture. It was fascinating for me that the biblical texts which stood out were not the "texts of terror" so often used against gays but rather the story of David and Goliath, the persistence of Bartimaeus in seeking access to Jesus even though the disciples wished him to be silent and kept at a distance (Mark 10:46-52), the "beloved disciple" still standing at the foot of the cross. Scripture was here being used for inspiration, not for the purposes of "feeling good about oneself" or justifying one's choices. His favourite gospel, he said, was John. The reason for this lay in the nature of its polemic, rooted in the disciples' quest to be faithful in a hostile world. So far as liturgy was concerned, it was the eucharist which was especially important to him. For a variety of sophisticated theological reasons, the words "This is my body broken for you" and the invocation to the Christ "who takes away the sins of the world" were close to the heart of his personal faith.

He said at our first meeting that he had no theology. My suggestion was that he did, that it was all there, just waiting to be prised out. I believed that if he were to do this, it would be very helpful to others in his position, and perhaps to the church at large in its own wrestling with these difficult, intimate issues. It was clear that he felt a great debt to feminist, black and liberation theologies, all of which had provided him with ways of articulating oppression. One effect of this was to make him sensitive to others who were likewise placed in the power of others.

We talked a great deal about power, especially the kind of power which someone in his position has. It may not seem obvious at first, and it is not sought-after power, but there still remains the power of choice. Given the difficult situation gay Christians face, it would be easier to walk away. It would be easier not to choose a public path which leads one to being stigmatized, feared and judged, often on the basis of rumour, hearsay and stereotype and in a way which ignores how an individual knows the love of God. He was also deeply aware of how we are all both oppressors and oppressed. This is part of our human condition, and to be made "in the image of God" is to be made for the purposes of life "in all its fullness".

In this kind of theology the doctrine of the incarnation is of central significance. This is the language of "embodiment"; it points to a God of vulnerable involvement rather than of abstraction and distance. With respect to ecclesiology, he said that if you are gay there must be a good reason to be in the church, whose homophobic history and public statements are alienating. There was a twist concerning forgiveness and repentance: the call was not so much upon the gay man or lesbian to repent and seek forgiveness or pastoral care; rather, it was the church itself which was being called to repentance. The viability of any genuine theology of reconciliation would depend upon that willingness to repent and to enter into the reality of those who have been stigmatized in the name of faith. Clearly our discussions had now brought us to some of the central themes of Christian theology. Significantly, these things were being thrown back, in effect, on the institution, as if it, rather than gays and lesbians, were being called upon to justify itself. I was left contemplating the nature of corporate and structural sin.

Embedded in the experience of being gay is a very rich theology, of which I have touched upon only some of its contours. And that is both a creative starting point and a source of frustration. It is difficult for a gay student to find his theological bearings at the best of times — and here were some conversations opening up great themes. There was depth and sensitivity. The frustration lies in the desire for more such conversations and the realization of how difficult they are at present in the formal life of our churches.

The point I would like to make is this: these conversations have enabled me to see the Christ in new ways in both biblical text and in liturgy — and rather than these readings being an act of special pleading, they strike me as radically orthodox.

Till Death Do Us Part

RALPH KNOWLES

"Why are you cast down, O my soul, and why are you so disquieted within me? Hope in God; for I shall again praise him, my help and my God" (Psalm 43:5).

My relationship of thirty years with my life partner David is drawing to a close. David has motor neurone disease (also known as amyotrophic lateral sclerosis or Lou Gehrig's disease) and is becoming weaker and weaker. Before long we will be parted for the first time in our adult lives. I do not know yet whether I will find the strength to continue living without him, since over the three decades we have been together we have become as totally interdependent as any married heterosexual couple.

It was clear to me by the time I was 11 years old that I was "different" from other boys my age, though it was some years before I realized the nature of the difference and the implications it would have for my life. We were all reaching adolescence and sexual awareness; my mates in the neighbourhood were becoming interested in women while I was secretly conscious from the first sexual stirrings that my "object of desire" was men. That sexual and affectional interest in adult members of my own male sex has been absolute and has not shifted at all over the years.

During a brief period of training for the Anglican priesthood, I submitted myself to aversion therapy, which was intended to eliminate my homosexual reactions and encourage heterosexual feelings. The treatment was primitive and barbaric and had little or no effect on my sexual orientation. Soon after I ended the therapy I met David, withdrew from theological training and began my life as a settled gay man living in a full social, domestic and sexual partnership with the man I love to this day.

My participation in the organized community of faith has waxed and waned over the years. Although I was brought up in the Anglican communion (in the catholic tradition), I converted to Roman Catholicism at a time when the Roman Catholic Church was opening up on theological and social issues. That process has since been reversed, and windows which were thrown open or at least unlocked have now been shut tight again. Today I associate with many Catholics — Anglican and Roman — and attend liturgies in both communions.

The only serious harassment David and I have experienced personally was from "Christian" people in the early stages of our relationship; and the fiercest opposition to granting human rights to gay people in Aotearoa New Zealand has come from "Christian" advocates. But in spite of that, I have never doubted that I was a loved child of God. Since I knew absolutely that I had not chosen my exclusively homosexual nature, I took it for granted that it was given by God. My tasks as a Christian were to love as I was loved, to live my life creatively and generously according to my Christian upbringing, to see Jesus Christ in others and to relate to them as I believe Jesus Christ might have done. Of course I am a sinner. Of course I haven't always accomplished those tasks fully. But my failures are common to all humans and have nothing to do with my being gay. While I repent of some of my behaviours and attitudes and regret particular things I have said or done (or not said or not done), I do not repent of being gay. I rejoice that God has given me such a blessing, such a rich life and such a wonderful life partner as David.

Our life together has had its share of ups and downs, misunderstandings and infidelities, but our love for each other provided such a strong foundation that the relationship has continued to grow in trust. We are committed to each other "for richer, for poorer, in sickness and in health, to love and to cherish, till death do us part".

Through all our years together we have enjoyed the good fortune of the understanding, friendship and support of both our families and of our friends and workmates. Our relationship has been respected as the equivalent (not the equal) of a marriage, and we have been included as a couple at family celebrations, official events and social occasions. The support has never been more evident than now when David's illness calls on more strength and resources than I alone can provide. Shortly after David's illness became known, a rumour started at work that he had AIDS. Both the management and unions made it clear that this was not the case and the rumour died. No one who matters has judged us for being gay or expressed embarrassment over the nature of our household. Health professionals, employers and other agencies have been very helpful to us and have discussed our situation and how we might cope with it without any obvious awkwardness about dealing with two men. Thank God for basic Christian charity.

This degree of acceptance by Christians and non-Christians contrasts sharply with the rejection, alienation and hatred exhibited by the officialdom of some supposedly Christian bodies during the campaign in the 1980s around the decriminalization of homosexual behaviour and the campaign in the early 1990s to include sexual orientation in the human rights act. Chief among the opponents of better treatment for gays and lesbians were the Salvation Army and the Roman Catholic Church. Pronouncements by the Vatican have become increasingly vicious and irrational. While many churches still distinguish between homosexual orientation and homosexual behaviour, viewing the first as morally neutral and the second as sinful, the Vatican has extended its negative comments to the homosexual inclination itself. In 1992 the Congregation for the Doctrine of the Faith declared that it is "overly benign" to consider homosexual orientation "neutral" since "it is a more or less strong tendency ordered towards an intrinsic moral evil". The Vatican also declared that it is not unjust to discriminate against people with a homosexual orientation in certain areas such as teaching, coaching, military recruitment, public housing and health benefits. The statement on homosexuality in the 1994 Roman Catholic catechism is brief: it condemns homosexual acts utterly; it is silent on homosexual orientation; and when it calls for discrimination to be "avoided", it carefully limits such avoidance to *unjust* discrimination (presumably as defined by the 1992 document). In my opinion, this limited definition of discrimination leaves the field for gay-bashing pretty wide open. Such a position is in stark contradiction to my understanding of what it means to be Christian. It is a curious stance for the Vatican to take in view of the fact that so many of the Catholic clergy in the Western world are practising homosexuals themselves. We have great sympathy with them in their perilous position and the double lives they lead.

All in all, I am happy to be a gay Christian and proud of my long-term relationship with David. Although I'm sad and stressed by his illness, I live in hope that we will both find the strength and support we will need to depart in peace. I believe that, in the Psalmist's words, God will send us light and truth and that after death there is "life in God". What form that life takes is unknown, but I live in confidence that love, whatever its source or focus, will continue to conquer all.